BUILDING FOOD
SECURITY

Canning, Dehydrating, and Freeze Drying

LORI ROETS VALONE

Building Food Security:

Canning, Dehydrating, and Freeze Drying

By Lori Roets Valone

Print ISBN: 978-1-7348824-8-3

E-book ISBN: 978-1-7348824-9-0

Library of Congress Control Number: 2022906172

Printed in the United States of America

Bacchus USA Publications, LLC

Post Office Box 599

Bryson City, NC 28713

BacchusUSAPublications.com

Dedication

I dedicate this book to my husband, Paul, who pushed me to "just get the words on the page". You may never hear me say it again, but you were right. Thank you for your ever-present love and support. It is wonderful to have writing as one of the many enjoyable pursuits we share. You had me before hello and will always have my love and respect.

I also dedicate this book to my mom, Carol. Thank you (and Dad) for instilling in me a strong work ethic and the discipline to get things done. I thank you most of all for ALWAYS being in my corner. I love you very much.

"There's no harm in hoping for the best as long as you are prepared for the worst."
- Stephen King

Acknowledgements

Thank you to these fine companies who gave their permission for the use their product images:

- Emergency Essentials (beprepared.com)
- HarvestRight (HarvestRight.com)
- Tattler Reusable Canning Lids (ReusableCanningLids.com)
- Pump-N-Seal® (Pump-N-Seal.com)

I heartily encourage you to support each of these great companies. All of their products are well worth the investment.

Thank you to Jan, Lacey, and everyone at Carolina Readiness Supply (CarolinaReadiness.com) in Waynesville, North Carolina. If you are looking for food, first aid, water purification, educational materials or anything else related to preparedness, check out Carolina Readiness in person or on the web. Teaching "Building Food Security" at their annual Heritage Life Skills (HLS) Conference is what drove me to write this book in the first place. I look forward to many more HLS in the years to come!

A heartfelt thank you to my beta readers – Jaci, Kathy, Shawna, and my mom, Carol – for their valuable feedback.

- Mom, thanks for being willing to be an alpha reader, shaping the early work.
- Jaci, your feedback on the worksheets and appendix were spot-on. Thank you!
- Shawna, I should have known you would be the only one to find the chicken faux pas! Good catch!
- And last, but absolutely not least, special thanks to Kathy for introducing me to pectin enzyme – I always wondered how they got all that white stuff off citrus. Now I know!

"Chance favors the prepared mind."
- Louis Pasteur

Table of Contents

PART ONE
Food Security 101

Chapter 1
Why Store?

Not since WWII have concerns about food security affected so many Americans. The ongoing shortages of basic food items on grocery shelves are a wake-up call for many who previously never worried about feeding their families.

There are as many different reasons for wanting to store food as there are foods to store. Life for our ancestors meant store or perish. The act of reading this book is testament to the fact that our ancestors were indeed masters of food storage. While the methods have evolved, the purpose remains the same.

Rural dwellers, and those with a patch of land big enough to grow a garden, typically store food without ever thinking about it. Let's face it. Unless you have a huge family or you are feeding an army, most gardens produce more than you can eat at one time. Even if you are a master of staggering your planting to optimize when food ripens, you will invariably have spoilage unless you store some of your production for later. More importantly, you need to store in times of plenty so you can eat during the long, cold winters. Most of the folks with substantial gardens do not even think about preservation as food storage. It is simply what they have done all their lives – what their parents and grandparents did. It is a way of life.

Of course, not everyone is blessed with a green thumb, gardening expertise, or even a bit a ground to plant. Thankfully, for some, food storage is not about feeding themselves but instead helping those less fortunate.

Perhaps the most prevalent reason for storing food is to prepare for natural disasters. The Federal Emergency Management Agency (FEMA) recommends storing two weeks of food and water for each family member to prepare for natural disasters.1 It should be noted that this guidance is a substantial increase over the three days of food FEMA used to recommend. You only need to look to the last hurricane, flood, ice storm, or forest fire for examples of why preparing for natural disasters is wise.

Not all disasters are natural. Pandemic. Cyberattack. Riots. Warfare. No one would have predicted the world would experience all of these non-natural disasters in a single year. In today's just-in-time world, stores no longer maintain a significant amount of stock on hand. Instead, they rely on replenishment from a regional

Food and Water in an Emergency

FEMA · American Red Cross
Together, we can save a life

Figure 1
Cover of FEMA brochure

warehouse, which is in turn relying on regular deliveries from suppliers. Most grocery stores maintain three or less days of stock on hand. When a supply chain breaks down because of natural or man-made disaster, it takes only a day or so for shelves to become bare.

During the COVID-19 crisis of 2020-2022, it became all too common to find empty shelves at the local grocery store. Living in a small rural town, I was surprised to discover the bread, produce, and meat sections of our only local grocery store absolutely and completely empty just a couple weeks into the worldwide health crisis. While it was only a frustration for me, those who only keep a few days food on hand – by either choice or necessity – were caught off-guard.

Before moving to my current mountain home, I lived on the outskirts of a major metropolitan area with two grocery stores within a half mile of my house. Now, the closest store is 25 minutes down a winding mountain road, and for anything more substantial, we must drive 40-90 minutes. As a result, we employ the Navy Seals' philosophy, **"Two is one, one is none"**, trying to maintain at least two of all key staples on the shelf. Adhering to this principle also provides some protection against another risk: price increases. As if the pandemic and supply chain constraints were not already enough, inflation piled on, further straining the ability of families to keep food on their tables. Food storage is an excellent hedge against both of these issues.

Long-term societal change is the reason cited by many of those who are storing food and other commodities. Storing a couple weeks' worth of food for a natural or man-made disaster pales in comparison to storing for the potential of months or even years of not being able to replenish food and supplies from a store. For those who believe society is heading toward the brink of disaster, food storage is their number one priority. These individuals will invest more time in long-term storage than those focused solely on meeting FEMA's two-week storage recommendation.

Meet the Smiths

Throughout this book, we will base our examples on a fictional family of five, the Smiths, living in mountainous, rural western North Carolina. John and Mary Smith are preparing for both short-term and long-term disasters.

While earthquakes, tornados, and hurricanes are not of primary concern where they live, significant winter storms are. Recent history has included epic snowfalls that shut down most transportation and commerce in the county for two weeks. Ice storms capable of snapping power lines like fine thread are also a known risk.

Figure 2
Fictional Smith family

The Smiths are even more concerned with the possibility of supply chain disruption, having seen food and gas shortages increase over the last year. Between riots, cyberattacks and a general change in the work ethic of the average American, the likelihood of long-term economic disruption seems to be looming closer and closer.

The present and growing potential for one or more of these events to occur has fueled the Smiths' desire to develop a food storage plan now. On the next page you will find the Smiths' *Why I Store* Worksheet.

You will find a blank copy of the *Why I Store* worksheet in the Worksheets section at the end of this book. You can also download a copy from my website, buildingfood-security.com. Think about the reasons your family wants to store food, and then complete your own worksheet. We will refer to this worksheet again in Chapters 3 and 21.

References

1.   "Food and Water in an Emergency", FEMA, accessed February 21, 2022, https://www.fema.gov/pdf/library/f&web.pdf.

WORKSHEET 1
Why I Store

Worksheet for: **The Smith Family**

I want to build food security for my family to *(check all that apply)*:

☐ Avoid having to go to the grocery store so often *(1-week supply)*

☐ Stretch my food dollars *(1-week supply)*

☑ Store the harvest *(no specific duration)*

☑ Prepare for natural disasters especially ___**winter storms**___ *(2-week supply)*

☑ Prepare for man-made disasters especially ___**cyberattacks**___ *(4-week supply)*

☑ Prepare for short-term supply chain breakdowns in my area *(4-week supply)*

☐ Prepare for price increase of foods my family needs *(2-week supply)*

☑ Prepare for economic unrest *(13-week supply)*

☑ Prepare for regional or worldwide pandemic *(13-week supply)*

☑ Prepare for long-term degradation of society *(1 - 2 year supply)*

☑ Prepare for the aftermath of an electromagnetic pulse (EMP) *(1 - 2 year supply)*

Chapter 2
For Whom Are You Storing?

Once you have established why you want to build your food storage, you will need to determine for whom you are storing. This set of individuals may be influenced by who currently lives with you, who may live with you in an emergency, and others you may want to help in a time of need. This set of individuals may also be affected by where you live, along with any food sharing agreements you may have established with others, such as a local preparedness network.

First and foremost, you will want to cover the needs of everyone in your immediate household. Any child over the age of 10 should be counted as an adult. The Mormons, well known for their emphasis on preparedness, recommend counting children 7-10 at 90% of an adult, children aged 4-6 at 70% of an adult, and children 3 and under as 50% of an adult.1 The Mormons also recommend adding one year to your child's current age before making this calculation since children's needs are constantly changing.

For example, consider a family of six with 2 adults, and children of 3, 6, 10, and 12 years of age.

First, we need to add one year to the age of each child to account for the fact that their nutritional needs are always changing. So instead of basing our calculations on children of ages 3, 6, 10, and 12, we will base it on children of ages 4, 7, 11, and 13.

Next, we need to figure out which age category each of the six individuals fit into. Our categories are 3 and under, 4-6, 7-10, and 11 and over. So, using the updated ages we just calculated, we have no one in the 3 and under group, one in 4-6, one in 7-10, and four in the 11 and over category.

Now, we apply the multiplier for each category. For the 4–6-year-old category we use a multiplier of 0.7. For the 7–10-year-old category, we use 0.9. There is no multiplier required for 11 and over.

Doing the math we get:

4-6	1 child x 0.7 = 0.7 of an adult
7-10	1 child x 0.9 = 0.9 of an adult
11 and over	= 4 adults

Adding these up, we get 5.6 adult equivalents.

By comparison, if we had not added the extra year onto the age of the children, we would have instead had one in the 3 and under category, one in 4-6, one in 7-10 and three in 11 and over. Doing the same math, including a multiplier of 0.5 for the 3 and under category, we get:

3 and under	1 child x 0.5 = 0.5 of an adult
4-6	1 child x 0.7 = 0.7 of an adult
7-10	1 child x 0.9 = 0.9 of an adult
11 and over	= 3 adults

This gives us 5.1 adult equivalents.

Planning for growing children will guide this family to store an extra half of an adult portion (5.6 adult equivalents – 5.1 adult equivalents) to meet the children's increasing nutritional needs. Therefore, this family of six should plan their food storage based on 5.6 adults, rather than 5.1 adults. Does your teenage son consume twice as much as his father? Does anyone have a very high metabolism? Add a little extra to cover these specialized needs.

Do you have children away at college, boarding school, or residential camp programs who might be home for a weekend or over a semester or summer break when disaster strikes? What about young adults or disabled adult children living independently nearby? Do not forget to account for their needs in your plan as well. Failure to do so will place a significant strain on your food supply if they are at home. Consider also whether or not your boarding school or college-aged child frequently brings home friends that may also need to be accounted for.

Do your parents or other family members live nearby? Are they storing adequately for their expected consumption, or will you need to store food to cover them as well?

Are you the designated rally point for family members who live somewhere else? If so, ask yourself these questions:

- Are you expecting arrivals to bring their full ration with them?
- Do they have sufficient space in their vehicle to carry their foodstuffs?
- Has their food storage been packaged to travel quickly?
- Moreover, what happens if they must travel on foot and cannot bring much of their food storage with them?
- Does it make sense to maintain a portion of their food storage at your location?

Unless you are 100% certain they will be able to make the journey to your location, they should probably hold on to a portion of their food supply at their primary location. It would be awful to know you had a year's worth of food stored – somewhere you are not!

For example, consider a family of two adults who are the rally point for their four children, two of whom are married. With only one of their children residing locally, it is prudent to estimate the percentage of their food they need to plan to provide as well as the probability their adult children will make it to the rally point. Children who live in distant locations, have jobs that might not allow them to leave, or who may have other family to consider should be counted with a lower probability than those who live nearby or those who have flexible lives. Those who will be with you throughout all or most of an emergency should be counted as if they require **full-time storage**. You will need to plan to meet 100% of their food needs. We will look at accounting for both probability and percentage of their food supply to store in more detail in the next section.

After you have evaluated your own family situation, consider others to whom you might want to provide assistance. Consider:

- Are their elderly or underprivileged families in your neighborhood who might need some help?
- Are you involved with a church or civic organization that routinely feeds a portion of the community?
- Are you supporting a long-term food bank to continue feeding those who depend on them?
- Are you part of a local preparedness network?
- Do you have any food sharing arrangements? Perhaps you are particularly good at growing potatoes and another member grows corn. Do you have a plan to trade?

Now consider the impact that where you live has on your food storage requirements. Do you live in a city or rural area? If you are in an urban area – such as New York City – where housing space is at a premium, storing food is likely to be a major challenge. If your studio kitchen is the size of a postage stamp, it is much easier to run to the store than to try to maintain a pantry of any size. Unfortunately, the fact that land does not exist in NYC except in city parks makes storing food that much more important. Growing your own in any quantity is not really an option. Live in a high rise? Your problem is compounded just by virtue of your proximity to all of your similarly constrained neighbors. What happens when they show up at your door, hungry?

Live in a suburban area? You may benefit from being able to grow some foodstuffs in your yard, but you also have neighbors a stone's throw away. Did they prepare or are they just going to "wing it"? Or worse, are they planning on taking yours?

If you are in a rural area, you likely have or can find a patch of land to grow a portion of your food – if you have the knowledge and the supplies to do so. It is also likely you will not have a neighbor right next door. Additionally, rural families are much more likely to store food, especially when the nearest grocery store is not just down the street.

Is your location a popular tourist destination? Tourists are not going to be prepared for anything but a good time. However, they will be hungry if the disaster du jour renders food outlets or stores unavailable. If they show up at your door, do you plan to provide them with any food or simply turn them away?

How often do you plan to provide assistance to individuals outside of your personal support group? Failure to consider this important question could have a detrimental effect on your ability to adequately feed your loved ones. Once you provide food to individuals outside your immediate circle, they may feel they can come back again and again, placing an unexpected drain on your supplies. You will do well to consider, in advance, what you are and are not willing to provide to outsiders. Are you willing to provide a single meal to anyone who shows up at your door? Three days' supply to a neighbor? What happens when what you have given your neighbor runs out? Will you turn them away?

Whom Are the Smiths Storing For?

Let's check in with the Smiths and see whom they are storing for. As you learned in Chapter 1, the Smith family consists of John and Mary and their three children: twins Jane and Lane (9) and 6-year-old Jesse. Adding a year to each of the children's ages puts them into the 7-10 range meaning each child should be calculated as .9 of an adult. This means that in their immediate family, the Smiths have 4.7 adult equivalent mouths to feed.

Mary's parents live next door and have already begun storing their own food supply. Mary knows that her parents are likely to have about 50% of what they need. This leaves the equivalent of 1 adult to still feed. Given that they live next door, there is 100% chance of them being present.

John's younger brother Jake resides in a nearby town with his wife, Susan and their 1-year-old son, Sam. They are not currently storing food. Since Sam is in the under 3 category, this family unit will need to feed 2.5 adults (1.0 + 1.0 + 0.5). However, since there is only a 90% likelihood that Jake, Susan, and Sam will make it to the Smiths' home, they can scale that back accordingly. (2.5 x .9 = 2.25)

Mary's sister, Mindy, and her husband, Chase, are urban dwellers and live 3 hours away. In the event of an extended disaster, such as the long-term degradation of society or the aftermath of an EMP, Mary's sister and her husband hope to be able to make it to John and Mary's house – the designated family rally point. They feel they have about a 75% chance of making their way to John and Mary's house, but will likely only be able to bring enough of their own food stores to meet 25% of their needs. If they make it, this will leave 1.5 adults to feed (1.0 - .25 + 1.0 - .25). Since there is only a 75% chance of Mindy and Chase making it, that can be scaled back. (1.5 x .75 = 1.125 adult equivalents)

Mary looks in regularly on their neighbor, Josephine, an elderly widow on a fixed income. Mary knows Josephine is not well prepared for a disaster and wants to be able to provide a couple of months of food, which we will refer to on the worksheet as storage duration (calculated as number of days divided by 365, in this case 60 days of food / 365 days = 0.164).

The Smiths live on five acres well off the main highway so they do not have the issues Mary's sister might experience in a big city, but they are in an area with a significant number of rental cabins. Clearly, vacationers are not coming prepared for a disaster. These individuals are likely to show up on John and Mary's doorstep looking for assistance. They have discussed how much support, if any, they would be willing to provide and have decided they would like to be able to provide three days of food for up to 15 people. This is the equivalent of .123 adults

The Smiths' *For Whom I Store* worksheet appears at the end of this chapter.

Based on their worksheet, the Smiths calculate they would like to be able to store enough food to feed 9.362 people per day. That is quite a few mouths to feed! If they feel they cannot possibly achieve this level of food storage, they need to reconsider the people, durations, and percentage of the food supply they are willing to provide. At a bare minimum, they need to plan to feed 4.7 adult equivalents just to cover the needs of themselves and their three growing children.

To better achieve their goals, can they increase the cooperative nature of their food plan? For example, can they arrange for Chase and Mindy to store a portion of their food supply at the rally point? Can they work with Jake and Susan to encourage them to begin storing whatever basic foodstuffs their budget will allow?

For Whom Are YOU Storing?

Now use the blank worksheet, *For Whom I Store*, in the Worksheet section at the end of this book to calculate the number of adult equivalents you want to build your food storage to support. Breaking your calculation down by immediate family, extended family, plus others to help can assist when tradeoffs are required. Covering the needs of your immediate family clearly comes first. Once you satisfy those needs, you can expand your food storage to cover extended family and, if means allow, others you want to help.

Calculating your food storage needs is not a one-and-done activity. You should revisit your calculation any time circumstances change that might affect the plan including:

- Birth or death of a family member or other individuals you plan to help
- Relocation (yours or another family member)
- Ability of others in your plan to meet their storage goals
- Your expectations for helping others

References

1. "Food Storage for One Year," *Ensign (The Church of Jesus Christ of Latter-Day Saints)*, March 2006, https://www.churchofjesuschrist.org/study/ensign/2006/03/random-sampler/food-storage-for-one-year.

WORKSHEET 2
For Whom I Store

Worksheet for: The Smith Family

Immediate Family
John and Mary (Parents), Jane (9), Lane (9), Jesse (6)

Age	How Many	Age Multiplier	Age Total
Adult (11+)	2	x 1.0	= 2.0
Children 7-10	3	x 0.9	= 2.7
Children 4-6	0	x 0.7	= 0.0
Children 3 and under	0	x 0.5	= 0.0
Immediate Family Total			= 4.7

Remember to add 1 year to each of the children's ages before placing them into an age category.

Extended Family
Mary's parents (50% of portion should be planned for, 100% likely to be present);
Jake & Susan and Sam, age 1 (100% of portion should be planned for, 90% likely to be present);
Chase & Mindy (75% of portion should be planned for, 75% likely to be present)

Age	How Many	Portion Multiplier	Age Multiplier	Likelihood Multiplier	Age Equivalent
Adult (11+)	2	x 0.5 (50%)	x 1.0	x 1.0 (100%)	= 1.0
Adult (11+)	2	x 1.0 (100%)	x 1.0	x 0.9 (90%)	= 1.8
Adult (11+)	2	x 0.75 (75%)	x 1.0	x 0.75 (75%)	= 1.125
Children 7-10	0				
Children 4-6	0				
Children 3 and under	1	x 1.0 (100%)	x 0.5	x 0.9 (90%)	= 0.45
Extended Family Total					= 4.375

Others to Help
Josephine (60 days); Ad-hoc people in need (3 days for 15 people)

Age	How Many	Support Duration (days / 365)	Age Multiplier	Age Total
Adult (11+)	1	x 60 / 365	x 1.0	= 0.164
Adult (11+)	15	x 3 / 365	x 1.0	= 0.123
Children 7-10	0		x 0.9	= 0.0
Children 4-6	0		x 0.7	= 0.0
Children 3 and under	0		x 0.5	= 0.0
Others to Help Total				= 0.287

Immediate Family __4.7__ + **Extended Family** __4.375__ + **Others to Help** __0.287__ =
Total adult equivalents on which to base your food storage ____9.362____

WORKSHEET 2 DISCUSSION

Immediate Family Section

Before we place the children into a category, we need to add one to each of their ages to allow for changes in their nutritional needs. This means the 9-year-old twins, Jane and Lane, will be counted as two ten-year-olds, and 6-year-old Jesse will be counted as a 7-year-old. As a result, we have three kids in the 7-10 category.

Completing the math, we will use a multiplier of 0.9 for our three 7-10 year-olds, giving us 2.7 adult equivalents for the children, plus 2 for Mr. and Mrs. Smith, yielding a total of 4.7 adult equivalents.

Extended Family Section

The calculation for the Smith's extended family needs to take into consideration the age of the family members, what portion of the food supply needs to be accounted for, and how likely the extended family member is to be there to use the food supply.

Mary's parents will definitely be there, so both the age multiplier and the likelihood multiplier will be 1.0. However, since they are bringing half their food supply with them, the portion multiplier for Mary's parents will be 0.5, giving a total of 2 people x 1.0 age multiplier x 1.0 likelihood multiplier x 0.5 portion multiplier, yields 1.0 adult equivalents for Mary's parents.

Jake, Susan, and Sam are 90% likely to be there but won't be bringing food with them so the Smiths will need to provide 100% of their calories. Our calculation becomes 2 people x 1.0 age multiplier x 0.9 likelihood multiplier x 1.0 portion multiplier, giving a total of 1.8 adult equivalents for Jake and Susan. We also need to add in Sam's calories (0.5 age multiplier x 0.9 likelihood multiplier x 1.0 portion multiplier or 0.45 adult equivalents, bringing out total for Jake, Susan, and Sam to 1.8 plus 0.45, or 2.25 adult equivalents.

Finally, Chase and Mindy will bring 25% of their food, so the Smiths need to plan for 75% and they are 75% likely to arrive. Our calculation becomes 2 x 1.0 age multiplier x 0.75 portion multiplier x 0.75 likelihood multiplier, yielding 1.125 adult equivalents for Chase and Mindy.

Therefore, the Smith's will need 4.375 adult equivalents to cover their extended family (1.0 + 2.25 + 1.125).

Others to Help Section

To provide 60 days of assistance to Josephine, the Smiths will need to plan for 0.164 adult equivalents (1.0 age multiplier x 60 days / 365 days support duration).

To provide 3 days of assistance for up to 15 people, the Smiths will need to plan for 0.123 adult equivalents (1.0 age multiplier x 3 days / 365 x 15 people).

The total adult equivalents needed is the sum of the 3 categories: 4.7 + 4.375 + 0.287 = **9.362**

Chapter 3
Calculating Your
Food Storage Goals

By now, you should have a good idea of how many people you actually need to store food for. Armed with this knowledge, it is time to begin considering the two other components of your food security equation: storage duration and calorie needs.

Storage Duration

While everyone would love to have one or more year's supply of food on hand, it simply is not practical for most families. Furthermore, food security is a journey. Unless you just won the lottery, you are not likely to go out and buy a year's supply of food all at once.

The first thing to consider is the minimum supply you would like to maintain at all times. I recommend you store no less than FEMA's recommended two-week supply. This is your first goal and one you should strive to attain as quickly as possible.

Next, consider your ideal food storage level. If you live in an apartment in an urban area, it is unlikely you will be able to grow your own food and therefore you will need to store to meet all of your requirements.

Maybe you have a patch of land to call your own, but do not know the first thing about gardening – you may still need to store all or most of your food. Now is a great time to start learning basic gardening skills so you can reduce your reliance on your food storage later.

If you are already an active gardener, you may be able to store some of your calorie needs and supplement with what you grow. Set a conservative estimate for the number of calories you can grow to allow for drought, insects, lack of time to work your garden, or other factors affecting your ability to grow, but plan to get your primary calories from food storage.

If you live on a farm, you are likely accustomed to growing a substantial portion of your food and can likely count on being able to cover a portion of your food needs with fresh produce, fruits, and perhaps even meat and eggs, supplementing with storage.

Determining Calorie Requirements

While in an extended emergency, you may be forced to reduce your caloric intake. I recommend basing your food storage on the normal daily calorie requirements you would follow in a non-emergency situation. By doing so, if you have more people than you expected, or circumstances dictate you will need to rely on your food storage for longer than you had originally planned, you will have built in a little leeway already.

So, what are ideal calorie requirements? Actual caloric demands depend on age, weight, metabolism, and level of physical activity. However, the United States Food and Drug Administration (FDA) suggests 2500 calories per day for an adult male of average size and moderate activity, and 2000 calories per day for a similarly active adult female, in order to maintain current body weight.[1] Calorie needs for children range from 1000 for children under 4 to 1600 for pre-teens. As activity increases, so will calorie needs. Keep in mind that, unless you already have a very active lifestyle, in an emergency you are likely to be expending more energy every day just to accomplish the necessities of life. Consider adding a few extra calories into your calories per day estimate to allow for the extra energy you will undoubtedly expend.

Using Basal Metabolic Rate (BMR) to calculate more accurate calorie needs

Estimates are generally good enough for the purpose of building food stores. If you want to calculate your daily caloric needs more accurately, use the Basal Metabolic Rate (BMR) method.

The **Basal Metabolic Rate (BMR)** is the number of calories it takes to sustain the body at rest. There are several formulas available, but the Mifflin-St. Jeor Equation is now considered the most accurate.[2]

Adult male BMR: (4.536 x body weight in pounds) + 15.88 x height in inches)
- (5 x age in years) + 5

Adult female BMR: (4.536 x body weight in pounds) + (15.88 x height in inches)
- (5 x age in years) - 161

To calculate your daily caloric needs based on your BMR, multiply your BMR by one of the following activity factors3:

- Little or no exercise: 1.2
- Lightly active (light exercise / sports 1-3 days per week): 1.375
- Moderate active (moderate exercise / sports 3-5 days per week): 1.55
- Very active (hard exercise / sports 6-7 days per week): 1.725
- Extra active (very hard exercise/sports plus physical job or 2X training): 1.9

Example: Mrs. Smith is 38 years old, weighs 138 pounds, is 5'5", and exercises twice a week.

Her BMR calculated as follows:

> 4.536 x 138 (her weight)
> + 15.88 x 65 (her height, 5'5" in inches)
> - 5 x 38 (her age)
> - 161
> = 625.968 + 1032.2 − 190 − 161 = 1307 BMR
> x 1.375 (multiplier for lightly active) = 1797 calories

This is the number of calories per day (1797) that Mrs. Smith needs to maintain her current. Clearly, as weight or activity level changes, so will her BMR and her daily caloric needs.

Estimating Daily Caloric Requirement for the Smith Family

Let's determine the daily caloric requirement for our fictional Smith family. In Chapter 2, we determined that, based on the number of people John and Mary Smith plan to feed, they need to provide food for 9.362 adult equivalents.

While you can certainly make a more exact calculation, we can estimate the number of calories we need per day by multiplying the number of adult equivalents by the number of calories for an adult, and choosing a calorie level appropriate to your group. If your group is all or mostly male, use 2500. If all or mostly female, use 2000. If your group is roughly 50-50, split the difference and use 2250. This number does not need to be exact but will give you a target to strive for.

While I do not recommend lowering this number, you might want to adjust it up if you are already very active, you are extremely overweight, or you are planning for a grid-down scenario where carrying out the basic activities of daily living will consume more calories that is does under normal circumstances. While losing weight is inevitable in an extended disaster, if you lose it all at once, it will compromise your long-term survival. Add a few calories (250 – 500) to offset the extra you are likely to consume. Clearly, children will use less than this daily number, but the excess will help provide for the true daily variation that will occur.

Since the Smith family is nearly evenly divided between males and females and is of average activity and physical size, we will use 2250 as our daily calories per person, yielding a need for 21,065 calories per day for their family unit to maintain current weight.

Let's break that estimate down into the three components we discussed in Chapter 2: immediate family, extended family and others to help.

Immediate Family	4.7 * 2250	= 10,575 calories per day
Extended Family	4.375 * 2250	= 9,844 calories per day
Others to Help	0.287 * 2250	= 646 calories per day

Only you can decide how you want to allocate your food storage, but I recommend working to achieve the needs of your immediate family first, then your extended family and only then look at potential aid to others.

Estimate Your "Calories to Store" Target

Now that we know the number of calories we optimally need to store per day to support those individuals we plan to provide food security for, we need only determine the duration for which we want to store in order to establish our total calories to store target.

While we want to calculate our total target, we also need to be realistic about our storage goals. Therefore, I recommend setting interim targets that will help you identify where you are on your food storage journey.

Using the Smiths as our example, let's look at the total duration and interim targets we want to calculate. To do so, we need to look back to the *Why I Store* worksheet completed in Chapter 1. Locate the event with the shortest probable duration and the event with the longest probable duration.

For the Smith family, the shortest duration event they are storing for is winter storms (natural disaster). The duration of winter storms will vary depending on if you are in Alaska, the upper Midwest, or the Deep South. The Smiths live in the mountains of Western North Carolina where winters can be bitter cold, snowy, and icy. While the typical duration is three to five days, there have been extreme storms in the last 30 years where no travel was possible for two weeks. Knowing this, the Smiths set their minimum storage duration at two weeks.

The longest duration event The Smiths have indicated they are concerned about is the aftermath of an EMP or, alternatively, the long-term degradation of society. We have no modern example of either type of event on which to base our estimate of duration to prepare for. Therefore, you will have to use your own judgement, but I would recommend planning for an event duration of no less than one year and ideally two.

With these timeframes and our daily calorie needs we can now calculate our storage goals using Worksheet 3, *How Much to Store*. A copy is available in the Worksheets section at the end of the book. The completed example *How Much to Store* worksheet for the Smith family is located at the end of this chapter.

As they begin their food storage journey, this worksheet shows the Smiths should try to store at least 141,750 calories. This calorie level would provide the Smiths' immediate family with 14 days of food at an average of 2250 calories per person per day.

In an ideal scenario, the Smiths would also like to provide for their extended family for two years, and they would like to be able to help a few additional individuals. This would require storing a whopping 15,048,950 calories! That is why it is essential to start small and develop some intermediate goals to work toward. It is very easy to get discouraged if you only focus on the ideal goal. Remember, ANY food storage is better than none. Start small and grow.

References

1. "Dietary Guidelines for Americans, 2020-2025", USDA, accessed August 31, 2021, https://www.dietaryguidelines.gov/sites/default/files/2021-03/Dietary_Guidelines_for_Americans-2020-2025.pdf.

2. Alastair Hazell, "BMR Formula (Basal Metabolic Rate)," The Calculator Site, December 4, 2018, https://www.thecalculatorsite.com/articles/health/bmr-formula.php.

3. "Eat Healthy: How Many Calories Do You Need?" Check Your Health, accessed January, 15, 2022, http://www.checkyourhealth.org/eat-healthy/cal_calculator.php.

WORKSHEET 3
How Much to Store

Storage goals for: <u>The Smith Family</u>
Calories per day for Immediate Family: <u>10,575</u>
Calories per day for Immediate and Extended Family: <u>20,419</u>
Calories per day for Immediate and Extended Family plus Others to Help: <u>20,615</u>

Minimum Storage Goal

Duration and for whom: <u>2 weeks (14 days) for immediate family</u>

Calories to meet minimum goal: <u>10,575</u> calories per day x <u>14</u> days = <u>148,050</u> calories

Ideal Storage Goal

Duration and for whom: <u>2 years (730 days) for extended family and others to help</u>

Calories to meet ideal goal: <u>20,615</u> calories per day x <u>730</u> days = <u>15,048,950</u> calories

---

Intermediate Goal 1

Duration and for whom: <u>2 weeks (14 days) for immediate & extended family</u>

Calories to meet int. goal 1: <u>20,419</u> calories per day x <u>14</u> days = <u>285,866</u> calories

Intermediate Goal 2

Duration and for whom: <u>30 days for immediate & extended family</u>

Calories to meet int. goal 2: <u>20,419</u> calories per day x <u>30</u> days = <u>612,570</u> calories

Intermediate Goal 3

Duration and for whom: <u>90 days for immediate family & extended family</u>

Calories to meet int. goal 3: <u>20,419</u> calories per day x <u>90</u> days = <u>1,837,710</u> calories

Intermediate Goal 4

Duration and for whom: <u>6 months (180 days) for immediate & extended family + others to help</u>

Calories to meet int. goal 4: <u>21,065</u> calories per day x <u>180</u> days = <u>3,791,700</u> calories

Worksheet 3 Discussion

First, transfer the calories per day calculated on the Smiths' Worksheet 2, *For Whom I Store*, for Immediate Family, Immediate and Extended Family, and Immediate and Extended Family plus Others to Help, into the blanks provided at the top of the form.

Minimum Storage Goal

Looking at Worksheet 1, *Why I Store* for the Smith Family, we see the event with the shortest storage duration is natural disasters, in their case, winter storms. The suggested duration to store for natural disasters is 2 weeks or 14 days. Since our initial storage goal is focused on the Smiths' immediate family only, we will use 10,575 as the calories per day on which to base our calculation. Multiplying this by the minimum 14 days storage for a natural disaster we get 148,050 calories to be stored to meet the Smith's minimum storage goal.

Ideal Storage Goal

Again, looking at Worksheet 1, *Why I Store* for the Smith Family, we find the event with the longest duration the Smiths are storing for is the long-term degradation of society or an EMP, both of which have the same recommended storage duration of 1-2 years. We will use two years for this example. Since the ideal storage goal includes providing for immediate family, extended family, and others, we will need to use 20,615 calories per day to cover the entire group. Multiplying by 730 days (2 years) yields 15,048,950 calories to be stored.

Intermediate Storage Goals 1, 2, and 3

Each of these three intermediate goals are based on meeting needs for the Smiths' immediate and extended family so all will be based on 20,419 calories per day. We will multiply this by 14 days, 30 days, and 90 days respectively to obtain our intermediate calorie goals as shown on the worksheet.

Intermediate Storage Goal 4

The Smith's final intermediate storage goal includes others to help so the calculation will be based on 21,065 calories per day. Multiplying the calories per day by the number of days (180) yields the Smith's fourth intermediate storage goal of 3,791,700 calories stored.

Chapter 4
Determining What to Store

Now that you have calculated how much to store for your family, the question is what to store. The answer: **It depends.**

While there are general guidelines on what to store (see sidebar), the most important guide in deciding what to store is what your family will eat. It does absolutely no good to store bananas and broccoli if your family will not touch them. Instead, think about what foods your family uses in a typical week.

To build your base stores quickly, consider buying bulk quantities of rice, oats, beans, and wheat. Such items are among those you are not likely to grow yourself. A 20-pound bucket of rolled oats (available for $70 at the time of publication) contains 101 one-cup servings, which equals 69 cents per serving. While you will not want a steady diet of oats – for many reasons – acquiring buckets of these staples is a quick and cost-effective way to build a storage base.

You cannot store too much rice. This versatile starch will give you energy in the form of carbohydrates. It is satisfying by itself, but more importantly, it can serve as a base or extender. Add fresh, canned, dehydrated, or freeze-dried meat and/or vegetables and rice becomes a complete meal. Add to soups. You can even grind rice into floor. Short on animal food? Add rice to stretch your pet food stores.

LDS Food Storage Recommendations

The Church of Jesus Christ of Latter-Day Saints (LDS), also known as Mormons, is well known for their emphasis on food storage. First, LDS recommends building a three-month supply of the foods in the family's normal daily diet.

Once a three-month supply of food has been established, the Mormon Church recommends focusing on long-term storage staples such as wheat, rice, oats, beans, and potatoes[1].

In addition, LDS recommends utilizing the guidelines published by Brigham-Young University's Department of Nutrition, Dietetics and Food Science in "An Approach to Longer-Term Food Storage"[2]. This one-page summary includes long-term storage items such as apples, onions, carrots, milk, and sugar, as well as shorter-term storage items such as cooking oils, spices, eggs, and yeast.

Increase your stored pantry painlessly by building "just one more" into your normal grocery trips. If your family loves green beans, when you see green beans on sale and are buying for everyday consumption, buy "just one" more and put it into your food storage. If you are on a strict budget, perhaps you can only add a few cans a month to your storage, but those will be a few cans more than you otherwise would have had in an emergency. Commercially canned goods have a shelf life longer than home-canned, but less than freeze dried food. While commercially canned foods may lose some of their nutritional value and taste over time, they can still provide calories long after their best-if-used-by date.

Let's take a look at that can of green beans you picked up at the store. The average can of cut green beans contains 3.5 servings. Each serving contains 20 calories so the entire can provides 70 calories toward your food storage goal. It is worth noting that a serving provides 1 gram of protein. No, it is not a lot, but given the cost of protein (which we will see in a moment), all sources of protein are valuable, no matter how small.

For comparison, consider a typical #10 can of freeze dried white meat chicken. This can from Emergency Essentials (BePrepared.com), my #1 commercial long-term food storage vendor, contains 24 half-cup servings and each serving has 120 calories.

We can estimate that 2.5 cups of dry chicken produces the equivalent of one pound of fresh chicken when re-hydrated. Since 2.5 cups is five half-cup servings, this can contains the equivalent of just under 5 pounds of chicken (4.8 lbs.) with a total of 2,880 calories per can. Just for the sake of illustration, let's imagine we were going to supply 2000 calories per day for one person for a year – 730,000 calories – only with chicken. With 2880 calories per can, it would take 254 #10 cans of chicken to supply our calorie

Freeze Dried

White Chicken

Emergency Essentials

24 servings per container

(equivalent to 4.8 pounds)

x 120 calories per serving

= 2,880 calories per can

INGREDIENTS: Chicken.

Processed in a plant that handles milk, wheat, egg, soybean, and tree nut products.

DIRECTIONS: Mix 1/2 cup of Freeze-Dried White Chicken to 1 cup of hot water. Let sit 5 minutes and drain off excess liquid. Yields 1/2 cup of white chicken to be used as you would regular cooked chicken.

NOTE: Oxygen removed by either nitrogen flushing or oxygen absorber. Absorber not for human consumption. Discard packet immediately upon opening!

STORAGE TIPS: Store can at a cool temperature. After opening, place the remaining food in a zip-top bag, squeeze out excess air, and seal. Place the bag back into the empty can and cover with the plastic lid. Remember: Heat, moisture, oxygen and light are common factors in food deterioration. Refrigerate or freeze reconstituted items in an airtight container.

Nutrition Facts

Serving Size: 1/2 Cup (24g) Dry
Servings Per Container: 24

Amount Per Serving

Calories 120	Calories from Fat 35
	% Daily Value*
Total Fat 4g	6%
Saturated Fat 1g	5%
Trans Fat 0g	
Cholesterol 60mg	20%
Sodium 70mg	3%
Total Carbohydrate 0g	0%
Dietary Fiber 0g	0%
Sugars 0g	
Protein 20g	

Vitamin A	0%	•	Vitamin C	0%
Calcium	0%	•	Iron	2%

*Percent Daily values are based on a 2,000 calorie diet. Your daily values may be higher or lower depending on your calorie needs.

needs. Obviously, we would never eat only chicken for a year, but it allows us to visualize just how much food storage we are actually talking about. Now let's consider this can of whole egg powder, also available from Emergency Essentials. Each serving provides only 80 calories but there are 72 servings providing a total of 5760 calories per can.

By comparison, if we were to exist solely on eggs for a year on the same 2000-calorie diet, it would only take 127 cans of whole egg powder to supply our calorie needs, approximately half as many as on our imaginary all-chicken diet above.

Emergency Essentials

Dried Whole Egg Powder

72 servings per container

(equivalent to 6 dozen eggs)

x 80 calories per serving

= 5,760 calories per can

INGREDIENTS: Eggs (whole eggs, less than 2% sodium silicoaluminate as an anticaking agent.

CONTAINS: Eggs.

Processed in a plant that handles milk, wheat, egg, soybean, and tree nut products.

DIRECTIONS: Mix 2 1/2 Tbsp. of Whole Egg Powder with 2 1/2 Tbsp. of warm water. Yields the equivalent of 1 large egg. Use for any recipe that calls for eggs. When using with other dry ingredients, it is not necessary to reconstitute egg. Simply add Whole Egg Powder to other dry ingredients and increase liquid measurements by necessary amount.

NOTE: Oxygen removed by either nitrogen flushing or oxygen absorber. Absorber not for human consumption. Discard packet immediately upon opening!

STORAGE TIPS: Store can at a cool temperature. After opening, place the remaining food in a zip-top bag, squeeze out excess air, and seal. Place the bag back into the empty can and cover with the plastic lid. Remember: Heat, moisture, oxygen and light are common factors in food deterioration. Refrigerate or freeze reconstituted items in an airtight container.

Nutrition Facts		
Serving Size: 2 1/2 Tbsp (12g) Dry		
Servings Per Container: 72		
Amount Per Serving		
Calories 80	Calories from Fat 50	
		% Daily Value*
Total Fat 6g		9%
Saturated Fat 2g		10%
Trans Fat 0g		
Cholesterol 210mg		70%
Sodium 60mg		3%
Total Carbohydrate 0g		0%
Dietary Fiber 0g		0%
Sugars 0g		
Protein 6g		
Vitamin A 2%	• Vitamin C	0%
Calcium 4%	• Iron	6%
*Percent Daily values are based on a 2,000 calorie diet. Your daily values may be higher or lower depending on your calorie needs		

No one is going to survive on chicken or eggs alone. In fact, my husband said he would not need 127 cans of eggs for a year because he would kill himself in much less time if he had nothing to eat but powered eggs!

Let's face it. Humans need variety, not just to satisfy their nutritional requirements but to satisfy their emotional needs as well. While life in an emergency is going to be anything but normal, having normal-ish food can help maintain mental well-being. Therefore, the first rule of food security is to store what your family will eat. The second rule is to store foods that will allow you to provide as balanced a diet as possible to ensure your family's nutritional requirements are met to the greatest extent possible.

The US Department of Agriculture (USDA) recommends the food balance depicted in their MyPlate. gov graphic.[3]

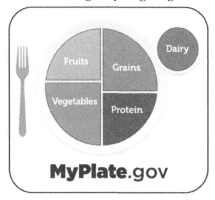

To achieve this balance consider storing food in accordance with the following ratios, to the extent possible:

- ❏ Proteins   20%
- ❏ Grains   25%
- ❏ Vegetables   25%
- ❏ Fruit   20%
- ❏ Dairy   10%

With this in mind, let's look in more detail at the foods that make up each of these five basic food groups.

Proteins

Proteins should be high on your storage priority list as they are essential to the body's function and repair capabilities. The USDA recommends that one-quarter of your daily diet come from proteins. In a balanced diet, the National Academy of Medicine recommends 0.8 grams of protein per kilogram of body weight, which equals about 7 grams per 20 pounds of body weight.[4]

Protein is built from a group of 20 amino acids, organic compounds that form the building blocks of life. Nine of these amino acids, referred to as essential, can be obtained only from food. A few foods, referred to as complete proteins, contain all 20 amino acids.

When most people think about proteins, they think about meat and perhaps beans. However, there are many other sources of protein available, and many are far less expensive than meat. While clearly, you are not going to be able to satisfy your protein needs solely with green beans or bananas, the protein in these foods do contribute to meeting your total daily protein requirements.

Protein Sources

- ▶ Beef, veal, chicken, pork, ham, turkey, lamb, mutton, goat, fish (fin or shell)
- ▶ Venison, elk, moose, bison, bear, rabbit, groundhog, opossum, squirrel, snake
- ▶ Eggs, milk, cheese, soy, quinoa – these are complete proteins
- ▶ Lentils, chickpeas, soybeans, most beans, green peas
- ▶ Wild rice, spelt, couscous, amaranth, buckwheat
- ▶ Nuts and nut butters, seeds (chia, flax, pumpkin, sesame, sunflower, squash)
- ▶ Tofu, tempeh, falafel, hummus

- ▶ Broccoli, spinach, asparagus, artichokes, Brussel sprouts
- ▶ Potatoes, sweet potatoes, corn, green beans
- ▶ Blackberries, nectarines, bananas

Grains

Another quarter of your diet should come from the grains group. While it is hard to store flour, meal, or finished grains (biscuits, bread, crackers, etc.), storing the base grains is easy and relatively inexpensive. Bulk wheat, rice, oats, quinoa, barley, buckwheat, bulgur, and cous-cous are readily available and store well. Flint or dent corn can

be also be grown. Make sure you have a manual or electric grain mill suitable to the types of grain you plan to grind. Corn, especially popcorn, is harder than other grains and may damage a standard grain mill. You can also store ramen noodles, which are made with wheat flour. While the standard shelf life of ramen noodles is about two years, they will remain good longer and make a good extender when mixed with other foods. If storing for long term, consider removing the seasoning packet and storing it separately from the noodles, as this is the portion most like to go bad. You can season the noodles yourself when rehydrating, if necessary. Ramen noodles are high in sodium so you do not want to overdo your reliance on them, but they are a very cheap source of grains.

Vegetables

Next up are the vegetables, which should make up more than a quarter of your diet – with more considered better. There are many, many vegetable options and almost all vegetables are suitable for long-term storage in one form or another. Fresh is best, but if fresh is not an option, commercially canned, frozen, home canned, dehydrated, or freeze dried are all viable choices.

As with all food types, store what your family will eat, but place your emphasis on calorie-dense or nutritionally high-value vegetables. In Appendix C, you will find a chart of vegetables with their calories per ounce to help you find the best calorie-dense choices for your family.

While garlic tops the list at 42 calories per ounce, unless you have a vampire problem, I do not suggest making garlic one of your primary staples, although it is a great choice to help add flavor to what can otherwise be some very boring meals! Similarly, olives, which come in at 32 calories per ounce, are not likely to make up a significant portion of your diet so you will not want to store a large volume of olives. Corn, however, is a great option at 27 calories per ounce, and also provides fiber to help digestion plus magnesium, potassium, phosphorus, and zinc.

One of the best choices? Good old peas! Not only are peas calorie-dense at 23 calories per ounce, but they are also relatively high in protein and a host of vitamins including C, K, E, and several B vitamins.[5] Vitamin C is particularly important, since survival diets are notoriously lacking in fruits, which are the prime source of vitamin C. Peas are inexpensive to store and can be used in many ways including as a simple addition to rice.

Potatoes are another good option, with sweet potatoes coming in at 24 calories per ounce and regular potatoes packing 22 calories per ounce.

You will certainly want to store or grow a variety of vegetables, not just those that are calorie dense. Variety is, after all, the spice of life as the old adage goes. Consider, also, any special dietary requirements. For example, if you are storing food for a diabetic you will definitely not want to focus your storage on the high-carb vegetables like corn, peas, or potatoes. Instead, you will need to focus more on the mid to low end of the spectrum. Beans, when used in moderation, can be a good choice. Cabbage, cauliflower, and eggplant are other good choices.

Fruits

Getting enough vitamins, especially C, can be a challenge in a survival situation. Apples are a great choice. They can be canned, dehydrated, or freeze dried. While we do not have an apple tree of our own, we are fortunate enough to live within an hour of a wonderful orchard and we typically put up two or more bushels of apples each fall. Between my young granddaughter and my husband, however, more than half of those never make it into long-term storage!

The potassium benefits of bananas are well known but they also provide vitamin B6, C, and magnesium. While you can't can a banana, they do dehydrate and freeze dry well.

Mangoes are a nutritional powerhouse and can be canned, dehydrated, or freeze dried. High in fiber, mangoes are also high in potassium, folate, and vitamins A, C, B6, E, and K.

Avocadoes are a calorie dense fruit, high in healthy fats. Low in sugar, they can be a good option for added calories for diabetics. Additionally, avocadoes provide potassium, fiber, vitamin B6, folate, plus vitamins E and K. As an added bonus, avocadoes contain lutein, which is important for eye health. Avocados can be freeze dried and are often stored as a powder which can be reconstituted to make guacamole.

A great source of vitamin C is pineapple, which is easily dehydrated or freeze dried. Pineapple is also a terrific source of manganese. Peaches, strawberries, and blueberries make excellent dehydrated or freeze dried snacks and all provide vitamin or anti-oxidant benefits. Keep in mind that the sugars are concentrated in dehydrated and freeze dried fruits, which can be either a blessing or a curse, depending on your need for calories.

Dairy

Rounding out the USDA MyPlate.gov recommendation is the dairy group. This can be the most challenging group to store, especially in respect to providing variety.

Unless you have a cow, goat, or sheep, you will need to store powered or freeze dried milk. Freeze drying can be a fantastic alternative if you need one of the specialty milks such as soy, almond, or oat milk.

Storing freeze dried cheese is another great way to satisfy your dairy requirements. A wide variety of sliced or shredded cheeses can be freeze dried and enjoyed directly or used in preparing other foods.

Yogurt is also another popular freeze dried item, either plain or blended with fruits or grains.

Balancing your Food Storage

Use Worksheet 4, *What to Store*, found in the Worksheets section at the end of the book, to calculate target calories in each of the five food groups as an aid when selecting items to store. Complete the worksheet based on your initial storage goal as calculated on Worksheet 3, *How Much to Store*. Deduct from this goal an estimate for the calories you will provide from fresh foods from your garden or from livestock. As you satisfy one storage goal outlined on Worksheet 3, complete a new worksheet to build for the next storage goal (e.g. intermediate goal 1, intermediate goal 2, etc.).

Think about the foods your family prefers to eat. Are there foods they find comforting in times of stress? Are there medical or dietary restrictions that must be considered? Use the food category columns at the bottom of the worksheet to list specific food items that satisfy the food storage needs of your group. Do not store all of one food group before moving on to the next. Be sure to store across all five food groups as you build your storage to ensure balanced nutrition.

The completed *What to Store* Worksheet for the Smith family appears on the next page.

References

1. "Food Storage," The Church of Jesus Christ of Latter-Day Saints, accessed March 31, 2022, https://www.churchofjesuschrist.org/study/manual/gospel-topics/food-storage.

2. "An Approach to Longer-term Food Storage," Department of Nutrition, Dietetics and Food Science, Brigham Young University, Revised September 2019, https://brightspotcdn.byu.edu/b1/4d/75fc449e4ce9843daa701f69faa4/an-approach-to-longer-term-food-storage.SEPT2019.pdf.

3. "My Plate," U.S. Department of Agriculture, accessed September 14, 2022, https://myplate.gov.

4. "What Should I Eat: Protein," The Nutrition Source, Harvard T.H. Chan School of Public Health, accessed April 2, 2022, https://www.hsph.harvard.edu/nutritionsource/what-should-you-eat/protein/.

5. "Vegetable Calories," Calories.info. Your calorie chart database: Calories for hundreds of foods, accessed September 15, 2022, https://www.calories.info/food/vegetables.

WORKSHEET 4
What to Store

Worksheet for: _____The Smith Family_____

Calculations for which storage goal: ____Minimum Storage Goal_____

Calories to store from *How much to Store* worksheet: _____148,050_____

Calculate target calories: Step 1: Calories to store x food category percentage = category total

                                  Step 2: Category total x (1 - percent of calories provided from fresh foods)

Protein (20%):   Step 1: __148,050__ x .20 = __29,610__
_0%_ **fresh**   Step 2: __29,610__ x (1 - _0.00_) = __29,610__

Grains (25%):   Step 1: __148,050__ x .25 = __37,013__
_0%_ **fresh**   Step 2: __37,013__ x (1 - _0.00_) = __37,013__

Vegetables (25%): Step 1: __148,050__ x .25 = __37,013__
_5%_ **fresh**   Step 2: __37,013__ x (1 - _0.05_) = __35,162__

Fruit (20%):   Step 1: __148,050__ x .20 = __29,610__
_1%_ **fresh**   Step 2: __29,610__ x (1 - _0.01_) = __29,314__

Dairy (10%):   Step 1: __148,050__ x .10 = __14,805__
_0%_ **fresh**   Step 2: __14,805__ x (1 - _0.00_) = __14,805__

Food Preferences to Store

Proteins	Grains	Vegetables	Fruit	Dairy
Chicken	Oats	Corn	Apples	Non-fat milk
Eggs	Flour	Peas	Peaches	Shredded cheddar
Ground beef		Sweet potatoes	Strawberries	
Red beans		Red potatoes		
Black beans		Cabbage		

Worksheet 4 Discussion

For this example, we are calculating the storage targets, by food group, to meet the Smith's minimum storage goal, copied from the Smith's Worksheet 3, *How Much to Store*, of 148,050 calories stored. Calculating the target calories for each food group is a two-step operation. First, we calculate the target calories for the food group. Then, we calculate the portion of that target which needs to be stored, after allowing for a <u>conservative</u> estimate of what we can provide from fresh foods from the garden, orchard or from livestock.

The Smiths are avid gardeners and, in the summertime, expect to be able to meet 15% of their calorie needs directly from their garden. However, since the natural disaster the Smiths are most concerned about is a significant winter storm, they will not be able to count on their garden to this extent, although they still expect to be able to cover 5% with fresh foods stored in their root cellar, such as cabbage and potatoes. Similarly, they only expect to be able to cover 1% of their fruit needs in the winter.

All five calculations will start with the goal of 148,050 total calories stored. Each group is calculated by multiplying by the USDA recommended daily contribution from each food group. For proteins (20% recommended), multiplying 148,050 by .20 (20%) we get 29,610 calories which should be provided by proteins. Since the Smiths do not expect to meet any of their protein needs from fresh food or livestock, the multiplier in step 2 would be 1 – 0 or 1. Therefore, we can skip step 2 of the calculation. The Smiths will need to store 29,610 protein calories to meet their family's protein needs over a two-week period.

Likewise, they will need to rely on storage for all of their grain needs, calculated to be 148,050 times the 25% recommended portion, or 37,013 grain calories to store for a two-week supply.

Accounting for the 5% of vegetable needs the Smiths expect to cover with fresh foods, we multiply 148,050 by the 25% recommended portion then multiply that result (37,013) by 1 minus the percentage fresh (5%) or 0.95. In other words, the Smiths will need to store 95% of the vegetables they need to meet the recommendation since they expect to only be able to provide 5% with fresh foods. This means they need to store 35,162 calories in the vegetable group.

Similarly, they will need to store 99% of their fruit needs (1 – 0.01). Since fruits should make up 20% of their diet, they will need to store 148,050 multiplied by 0.20 then multiplied by 0.99, or 29,314 fruit calories.

The Smiths will need 148,050 total calories multiplied by 0.10, or 14,805 calories, to meet the recommended 10% of calories from dairy requirement. Because the Smiths will provide 0% of their dairy needs, we can skip step 2, leaving them with the 14,805 calories calculated in step 1.

Finally, the Smiths have listed the foods to store in each of the five food groups. This will help them figure out how much of each food item to store, depending on the calories each type of food provides.

Chapter 5
How to Store

In Parts Two, Three, and Four, you will learn how to render fresh, canned, and frozen foods shelf-stable so they can be stored for as much as twenty-five or more years. But, even more important than the preparation of food is how you package and store them. Moisture, oxygen, temperature, and light are the bane of food storage. Therefore, it is important to use packaging and storage methods that protect from all four. The specific packaging and storage techniques used for a given food will depend on the preservation method you use, and how long you plan to store the food item.

I strongly recommend rotating your storage – using items and replacing them, especially those with a shorter shelf life. This will enable you to sample the foods you have stored to verify how well they store, how well you can incorporate them into meals, and how well your family will eat them. Do not invite a crisis the first time you use dehydrated or freeze dried foods to prepare a meal.

Packaging for Short-term Storage

Home canned food will always be stored in glass jars of varying sizes. Properly sealed canning jars protect against air and the microbes air brings with it. Moisture itself is not a problem with canning (except in the case of dry canning which we will not cover in this book). A root cellar or cool basement, away from light and heat, is the ideal location to store your home canned food. Make sure the shelves on which you store your canned goods are sturdy to avoid accidental breakage. If you do not have a dark, cool storage location, store in a cupboard, away from your stove or oven, to at least minimize exposure to light and heat. We will discuss canning in depth in Part Two.

Foods which have been dehydrated or freeze dried and are planned for short-term use may also be stored in canning jars if packaged with an oxygen absorber. This is one place you can reuse all those lids left over from canning. Inspect them to be sure the seal is still intact before using. The same considerations outlined above for home canned foods also apply to dehydrated and freeze dried foods stored in canning jars.

I strongly recommend vacuum sealing any jars used for short-term storage to guard against moisture and air. Two methods are available to vacuum seal canning jars. The first requires a FoodSaver or other vacuum sealer that supports a jar-sealing accessory. Jar-sealing accessory kits come with sealers for both regular and wide-mouth canning jars, along with a hose to connect the sealer to the vacuum unit. To use, place a canning lid on the jar, place the correct size sealer over the lid, and run the food sealer on the correct accessory setting until a vacuum is formed. This is quick, easy, and painless, and works for as long as you have power.

I have heard of owners who used the vacuum cycle on their freeze dryer to vacuum seal their jars. However, I have also heard of cases where the jars shattered while being processed this way. Therefore, I do not recommend using a freeze dryer to vacuum seal jars. That is simply not the job that freeze dryers were designed to do.

four steps TO FRESHNESS

Figure 3
Pump-N-Seal® (pump-n-seal.com), manual vacuum sealer

My preferred method of vacuum sealing jars is with a hand-operated device that will work grid up or grid down: the Pump-N-Seal® (pump-n-seal.com). A small hole is punched in one of your canning lids. Previously used lids, in good condition, are perfect for this! A small Band-Aid® looking item known as a Tab-Chek™ valve is applied over the hole you created in the lid. This simple solution allows you to vacuum seal by pressing up and down on a spring-tensioned device, creating a vacuum by hand. This process draws the air up through the small hole in the lid, which is then sealed by the Tab-Chek™ valve when a vacuum is created. The beauty of this device is the fact that you can quickly open and reseal jars, maintaining the quality of your dehydrated (and freeze dried) foods. In my opinion, everyone should have one of these little gems. Even if you are not currently dehydrating or freeze drying, you can use this wonderful tool to vacuum seal in canning jars, foods that often get stale, such as crackers, croutons, vegetable crisps, or foods which are susceptible to moisture incursion like flour, sugar, or cornmeal.

Packaging for Long-term Storage

Long-term storage of dehydrated and freeze dried foods requires the use of Mylar® bags. Mylar® is a polyester film developed by DuPont that is strong, puncture resistant, and impermeable to light, air, and moisture. Mylar® film itself is transparent. A thin aluminum layer is applied to the film to provide an oxygen barrier. While most bags tend to be silver, the aluminum film can be any color.

There are numerous manufacturers of Mylar® or Mylar-like bags in varying thicknesses. Beware of bags made in China offered for extremely cheap prices – they are typically thin and may not provide the expected protection. In general,

Figure 4
Three sizes of Mylar® bags

look for bags that are at least 4.5 mils thick, with 7 mils providing optimum protection. Mylar® bags come in a wide variety of sizes. I recommend having several sizes available so you can match the bag to the food and usage. If you are storing herbs and spices, you only need a small bag. If you are storing apples or other dimensional items, you will want a larger bag such as 10″ x 14″ (one gallon) or even 12″ x 18″. The two bags I use most often are the quart (8″ x 12″) and 5″ x 7″, a size particularly useful for a single serving. Do <u>not</u> use clear or windowed bags for long-term storage, as one of the purposes of a Mylar® bag is to keep out light. I found myself with more 12″ x 18″ bags than I needed so I cut some in half, creating two 6″ x 9″ bags that were just perfect for many foods.

Mylar® bags are sealed with an impulse sealer, which applies a thin band of heat while pressing the two sides of the bag together, fusing the film to create an air-tight seal. You cannot seal Mylar® bags with a vacuum sealer. Impulse sealers can be found on Amazon and other retailers from about $30 up. Make sure the width of the sealer you choose is more than the width of the largest bag you plan to seal. When cutting a bag in half, as described above, you will need to seal BOTH ends of the bag with the impulse sealer, not just one.

Figure 5
Impulse sealer used to seal Mylar® bags

Before sealing, you will need to place one or more oxygen absorbers into each bag. The number depends on the size of the bag, the size of the oxygen absorber, the quantity of food placed into the bag, and the density of the food item stored.

Figure 6
Oxygen absorbers, as delivered and stored in air-tight container

Oxygen absorbers contain the same material found in popular hand warmers, an iron powder that becomes iron oxide when exposed to oxygen, trapping the oxygen from the adjacent environment. As this chemical reaction occurs, small amounts of heat are released.

Oxygen absorbers come in sizes from 50cc to 2000cc. Refer to the chart in Appendix D for the recommended volume of oxygen absorbers to include for common bag sizes. I highly recommend finding a supplier that packages their oxygen absorbers in sets of ten. This allows you to expose only a few to air at a time. Oxygen absorbers are very good at their job. As soon as you open the outer packaging, they go to work. If you open a package of 100 oxygen absorbers that is not sub-packaged in smaller units, they are likely to be expended long before the time you want to use them. When I open a package of ten, I store my unused packets immediately in a half-pint mason jar.

To illustrate, in a 6" x 10" bag (1/4 gallon), use 100cc of oxygen absorber capacity for dense foods and 100-200cc of oxygen absorber capacity for less dense foods. Most dehydrated foods will fit into the less dense category. Examples of dense foods are wheat, flour, rice, and grains. I recommend buying primarily 100-300cc oxygen absorbers and using multiple packets to achieve the desired oxygen absorber volume. You can use a larger oxygen absorber (e.g. 500cc or 1000cc), but when used in a smaller package this large packet will be overkill. On a 1-gallon bag, only 300-400cc is required, so even a 500cc packet is more than necessary. You are paying for capacity you do not need. By using the smaller packets, you achieve the same goal while maintaining the best flexibility. The one place that larger volume oxygen absorbers are useful is packaging foods, such as rice, beans, wheat, or sugar, directly into buckets. In this case, there is likely to be more oxygen that may need to be removed from the enclosed space and a larger volume oxygen absorber will be well-equipped to do the job.

As the oxygen absorber pulls oxygen out of the bag, you may notice the Mylar® conforms to the food in bag as was the case with the chicken on the right in Figure 7. Do not be alarmed if this does not occur, as shown with the chicken on the left in the same figure. It does not mean your oxygen absorber is bad or that your package will spoil.

Be sure to label your Mylar® bag with the food inside, the date stored, and information on number of servings or amount of food, if available. If the food item is one that may be stored either dehydrated or

Figure 7
Chicken stored in Mylar® bag, sealed with impulse sealer

freeze dried, I would advise distinguishing freeze dried foods from dehydrated – I typically just use the abbreviations DH (dehydrated) and FD (Freeze dried). I speak from experience when I tell you it is easier to write on your bags before you add the food, although it can be done afterward (albeit not as neatly). You can also use a label maker to print labels.

Selecting a Storage Location

Select a storage location that is dry and cool, but not subject to freezing. This typically means storing in conditioned (heated, cooled and humidity controlled) space, when possible. Garages, sheds, and attics are not great storage locations, especially if you live in a hot or humid region. Avoid clear packaging and storage containers (when possible), except for short-term storage or when required by the preservation method, such as in the case of canning. Seal well and take precautions to prevent moisture damage. Make sure to take steps to prevent insects, rodents, and other pests from getting into your storage containers. Check frequently for any signs of pest activity and renew your protection methods regularly.

As you will quickly discover, it does not take too many Mylar® bags before these packages become unwieldy due to their irregular shape and size. You will need a way to contain and organize them. Some use buckets, while others use boxes. I have found large plastic bins to be the best choices for me. I chose bins tall enough to handle my largest Mylar® bags without a lot of wasted space. Additionally, I looked for a length and width capable of holding at least two rows of food, side by side, when the bags were standing upright. In reality, it is difficult to maintain rows due to differing heights and thicknesses of the packaging. If space is at a premium, look at plastic containers designed to fit under beds. Here, you may be forced to use clear containers as I do not believe I have ever seen these made in opaque materials. However, since the purpose is to fit them under the bed, light will be at a minimum

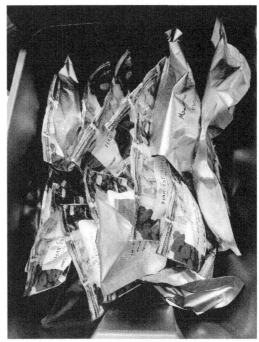

Figure 8
Mylar bags of food in an open storage bin

anyway. Your Mylar® bags already provide light protection. Using an opaque container is simply a secondary line of defense. You may need to get creative to find locations to store your food and to find containers that fit your storage locations.

Figure 9
Labeled food storage bins

Consider using a variety of bin colors to color-code your foods, such as, proteins and complete meals in blue bins, vegetables in green, fruits in yellow, etc. This can make it easier to add new items and to find what you need quickly. My granddaughter loves my freeze dried fruits, especially the apples, and I frequently get calls to send more. Color-coding would allow me to narrow my search for apples to a few selected bins. Unfortunately, the recent supply chain crisis has greatly restricted the available choices, so, for now, all my bins are teal. As supply chains improve, I will seek to add additional colors to my bins to implement color-coding.

Label your bins well. I recommend applying a label on all four sides and on top. This will allow you to determine what is in the bin, no matter where it is sitting. I invested in a label maker that allows me to quickly and easily make labels for both my canning jars and my storage bins. Make sure you buy plenty of extra tape cartridges for the label maker you choose. If you do not have a label maker, print or hand-write your labels on plain paper, then cut and apply to the bins with clear packing tape. Make sure the surface is clean and dry before you put the labels on to maximize adhesion. There is nothing more annoying than discovering your labels have fallen off and having to search multiple bins for the food item you are looking for.

Keeping Track of What You Have

You can further expedite your search for a specific food item by including an inventory sheet in each container, like the one in Appendix A or available for download from buildingfoodsecurity.com. Simply place a blank form in the container and handwrite each addition as you place it in the bin. Be sure to write neatly since it might be someone other than yourself who needs to retrieve items from the container.

Additionally, you should add each new item stored to your master inventory log. The master inventory log will be your comprehensive guide to what you have stored and its contribution to your nutritional and caloric goals. A sample Master Inventory Log form is available in Appendix B. If possible, you will want to maintain this log (or a copy) as an electronic spreadsheet so you can easily tally your inventory, printing copies regularly to ensure you have a copy if your computer becomes disabled. A Master Inventory Log template is also available for download from my website at buildingfoodsecurity.com.

Make sure, when you use items from your inventory, to update both the container inventory sheet and the master inventory log. Otherwise, you will wind up thinking you still have items in inventory that you have previously consumed!

Compare your calories on-hand to your storage goals at regular intervals to ensure you stay on track. Adjust your storage activities to ensure adequate coverage of the five food groups, especially as you rotate your storage.

PART TWO
Canning

Chapter 6
What is Canning?

Figure 10
Pantry filled with home-canned goods

Canning is a food preservation method that uses the application of heat to create a hermetic (complete and airtight) seal on cans or glass jars, thus providing a sterile environment in which harmful bacteria are unable to grow. The canning process involves placing foods in jars and heating them to a temperature that destroys microorganisms that could be a health hazard or could cause the food to spoil. Canning also inactivates enzymes that could cause spoilage.

Heating drives air from the jar, and as it cools, a vacuum seal forms. The vacuum seal prevents air from getting back into the product, bringing with it microorganisms to recontaminate the food. While both commercial and home canning use a similar approach, there are major differences between the two.

Commercial canning uses industrial equipment capable of achieving higher temperatures and pressures than can be achieved in home canning. The commercial canning process is carefully controlled to ensure the final product meets the exacting standards of the US Food and Drug Administration (US FDA). As a result, commercially canned foods have a longer shelf life. While most commercially canned foods have a best-by date within 1-2 years, canned foods have been proven to be safe to eat as much as 109 years after they were canned! In 1865, the steamboat Bertrand sank in the Missouri

River, loaded with provisions being delivered to a gold mining camp. The ship was recovered from under 30 feet of sand in 1968, and in 1974, the National Food Processors Association (NFPA) decided to test the brandied peaches, oysters, plum tomatoes, honey, and mixed vegetables recovered from the wreckage. While the food no longer looked and smelled fresh, the testing revealed no microorganisms and the NPA deemed the food just as safe to eat as it was when packaged in 1865 or

Figure 11
Commercial canning operation

before. They also tested a 40-year-old can of corn that not only was safe to eat, but also still smelled and looked as if it was fresh canned.[1] And in 2015, polar explorers found and ate combat rations in metal tins dated 1955 and 1960. The tins contained crackers, jam, cocoa powder, meatballs, and beans, all still in edible condition.[2]

Home canned goods, by comparison, have a shelf life of 1-5 years. The chief concern with home canning is safety, as improperly canned foods bring with them the risk of the potentially fatal illness, botulism, caused by the bacteria *Clostridium botulinum*. Since safety hinges on the correct application of time and, in some cases, pressure, to a specific type of food, it is critically important to use only canning recipes which originated from a trusted source, such as the USDA or other authority on canning. Additionally, reusing lids is highly discouraged as there is an increased likelihood of seal failure. Any home canned jars that fail a seal test taken at 24 hours after processing should be refrigerated and used within two weeks. We will cover this in detail in Chapter 9.

References

1. Dale Blumenthal, "The Canning Process: Old Preservation Technique Goes Modern", FDA Consumer, September 1990, https://web.archive.org/web/20190209185848/https://www.questia.com/read/1G1-9009146/the-canning-process-old-preservation-technique-goes.

2. Danny Lewis, "Artic Explorers Uncover (and Eat) 60-Year Old Food Stash", Smithsonian Magazine, October 22, 2015, https://www.smithsonianmag.com/smart-news/arctic-explorers-uncover-60-year-old-food-stash-180956936/.

Chapter 7
Canning Tools and Methods

The primary tools for canning are simple. Regardless of which canning method you use, you will need glass jars, lids with gaskets, and metal rings to secure the lids. Additional tools will vary based on the food you are canning and the method with which you choose to can.

Canning Jars

Jars comes in a variety of sizes and styles. They can be reused unless the glass is cracked or the top edge, known as the lip, develops chips. It is important to inspect the top of all jars closely before filling to make sure there are no defects, as small imperfections can cause the jar to experience seal failure.

Figure 12
Lid and ring - Regular (left) and Wide-mouth (right)

Two openings, more commonly referred to as mouth sizes, are available. Some jars are only available in one mouth size, while others offer a choice. Regular mouth jars have an opening of 2 ¾". Wide-mouth jars have a mouth of 3 3/8".

Standardizing on a mouth size, where possible, can make it easier to buy canning lids. Personally, I prefer wide mouth jars for my pints and quarts because they are easier to fill. I do have to maintain a smaller supply of regular lids for my quarter-pint and half-pint jars and those few assorted jars I obtained before I realized the value of standardization.

Figure 13
Pictured (left to right): Quart wide-mouth, quart regular-mouth, pint wide-mouth, pint regular-mouth, half-pint regular-mouth

Typical jar sizes and their uses include:

- **Quarter-pint** *(regular mouth):* 4 ounces for jams, jellies, preserves, and relishes
- **Half-pint** *(regular mouth):* 8 ounces for jams, jellies, preserves, and relishes
- **Three-quarter-pint** *(regular mouth):* 12 ounces for jams, jellies, preserves, relishes, sauces, fruits, and vegetables
- **Pint** *(regular and wide mouth):* 16 ounces for jams, preserves, relishes, fruits, vegetables, and meats
- **1.5 Pint** *(wide mouth):* 24 ounces for longer vegetables such as asparagus, cucumbers, and long beans
- **Quart** *(regular and wide mouth):* 32 ounces for fruits, vegetables, meats, one-dish meals, and soups
- **Half Gallon** *(wide mouth):* 64 ounces for very acidic fruit juices

Figure 14
Embossed (left) and smooth (right) jars

The smaller sizes (quarter-pint and half-pint) are available in both plain and quilted styles. Pints and quarts come embossed with a fruit motif or with smooth slides. The quilted or embossed glass adds form rather than function, but can be a nice touch for gift giving. All styles are equally effective. The choice is yours.

In the United States, Newell Brands holds the license from Ball Corporation to manufacture jars and supplies under the brands Ball and Kerr, two household names dating back to the 19th and early 20th centuries. Ball-labeled products are available predominantly in the Eastern US, while Kerr products are found predominantly in the Western US.[1] Ball products are also available in Europe along with Weck, Leifheit, and Kliner. While Leifheit and Kliner mason jars are similar to Ball jars, Weck uses a different design and is *not* USDA approved for use in the United States.

Traditional Canning Lids and Rings

You may have seen vintage canning jars with glass lids held on by a simple wire mechanism. This style was used until 1903 when Alexander Kerr introduced flat metal lids with an attached rubber gasket. With some additional improvements introduced in 1915, this style of lid remains in use today. The most notable exception to this is the Weck jar from Germany, mentioned in the last section, which is closer to a vintage canning jar than a modern one.

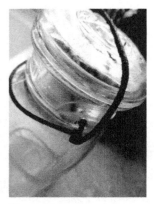

Figure 15
Vintage canning jar

Modern canning lids are discs of tin-coated steel with a thin food-grade coating applied to prevent corrosion from the contents. Since 2013, all Ball and Kerr lids have been BPA (bisphenol-A) free. BPA, once used in this coating, was rumored to cause cancer and other health issues, but further research has not borne out these rumors. The edge of the disc has a permanently installed rubber gasket that fits the lip of the jar to create the hermetic seal. A metal screw ring completes the closure system. You will also see one-piece plastic screw-on lids, advertised as leak-proof. While, these lids are great for use once you open a jar of food you have previously canned, they are not suitable for use during the canning process. I do keep a few of these types of lids on hand, as they offer faster closure on often-opened jars.

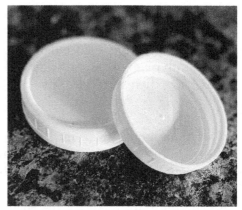

Figure 16
Screw-on lids - wide-mouth (left)
and regular (right)

While rings can be reused many times, traditional canning lids must be replaced each time. The heating process has the potential to damage the thin rubber gasket preventing a vacuum seal from forming if reused. Nonetheless, there are individuals who do reuse their lids and certainly, if faced with complete unavailability of lids, it might prove necessary to do so in order to preserve the harvest.

New jars come with lids and rings. This is how I acquire most of my rings. Periodically, I will also pick up a dozen replacement rings with lids. You should inspect rings prior to use and discard any with visible rust or dents. Contrary to common belief, storing finished jars with the ring in place is not recommended, although many people, including myself, often do it. The only purpose for the ring is to hold the lid in place until a vacuum forms. After 24 hours, you should remove the ring and wash it. It is not necessary to leave the ring on your jars after the 24 hours have passed. You can return the ring to service, and, in this way, a relatively small number of rings can cover all your canning needs. If you do decide to store with the ring in place, make sure it has been removed, washed, and replaced. Do not store a jar with the ring in place without washing.

Both jars and lids became scarce during the worldwide COVID-19 pandemic of 2020 – 2022, highlighting the importance of maintaining an adequate supply. While I had enough jars (in my opinion, more is always better!), I would have preferred to have had more lids on hand. Lids are sold by the dozen and do not take up much space. I would much rather have too many than too few. I wound up paying a king's ransom for lids on Amazon to ensure I had more than enough available for the 2021 harvest. Having standardized on wide-mouth jars made my search slightly easier, as I only had to search for one size lid.

The rubber gasket on each lid does not have an infinite life. It has been suggested that lids should be discarded after five years. I recommend keeping track of when you acquired your new lids and use them in FIFO (first in, first out) order.

I do save all my used lids. Why? Because although used lids are not recommended for repeat canning, they are just fine to use for short-term storage of non-canned goods. For example, I store dehydrated and freeze-dried items I expect to use in the next month or so in canning jars with used lids. I have not had any issues with foods going bad when stored in this way. You should inspect the lid for obvious damage before using.

So, what happens if you simply cannot buy any more lids due to a pandemic or other supply chain issue? This is the second reason I keep all my old lids. Should you run out of new lids, you could make a conscious decision to reuse lids. The issue is how well the thin rubber gasket will be able to seal a jar a second time. Canning causes an indentation in the shape of the jar top to form on the gasket. If this indentation does not perfectly align with the next jar top or if the gasket has thinned out more in one spot than another, a failure to seal may occur. If you make the choice to reuse lids, you must expect a higher than normal failure rate and be extra-diligent in checking the seals, not just when canning is completed, but also in the future as these lids may be more susceptible to seal failure later on as well.

Some canners do routinely reuse lids, especially if they live in areas where supplies are difficult to obtain. Autumn, author of the blog *"A Traditional Life"*, shared her process for reusing lids. After inspecting carefully for imperfections in the rubber gasket or the lid itself, she thoroughly washes those lids that pass muster in hot soapy water to ensure any residue from previous canning is removed, and then boils the lids for 20 minutes. She reports the process of extended heating makes the rubber more pliable and allows it to lose some, but not all, of the indention from the prior jar. She allows the lids to cool and dries them before using. She also notes this process typically works only once, is not ideal for jams and jellies which have very short canning times, and is less reliable for items to be pressure canned.[2] While I have not used this method, I would absolutely try it if I did not have access to new lids. Use with care and at your own risk.

Indefinitely Reusable Lids

There is, however, one type of lid designed for reuse. Loren Stieg invented Stieg Tattler Reusable Canning Lids in 1976 when faced with a similar shortage of metal canning lids. Rather than the traditional two-piece design, Tattler Reusable Canning Lids use 3 pieces, with the rubber gasket separate from a plastic (rather than metal) lid. Tattler lids are made to be used indefinitely – once you buy them, they never need replacing. The rubber gasket (seal) will last approximately 12-15 years with

Figure 17
Tattler, the original reusable canning lids from Stieg

44

proper care. Replacement gaskets are available from the manufacturer. Metal canning jar rings (bands), which hold the reusable lid and seal to the canning jar, are purchased separately.

Tattler lids did not become popular until 25 years after their initial introduction. While Tattler Reusable Canning Lids never went out of business, in 2010, Stieg saw the opportunity to begin manufacturing the product once again. Widespread use of both the internet and social media have helped to spread the word of their existence to the canning world. While at least one knock-off is available, Tattler (reusablecanninglids.com) remains the standard in reusable lids.

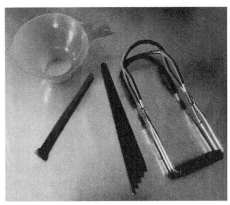

Since the rubber gasket is separate from the lid, the instructions for using Tattler lids differ slightly from traditional lids, most notably in the fact that the lids need to be left a little looser while canning is taking place and tightened, while still hot, after removal from the canner. This allows the air to vent as it would with traditional one-piece lids. With this adjustment, results are identical to traditional lids, with the benefit of reusability. The trade-off is initial cost, as indefinitely reusable lids and their companion gaskets are about twice the price of traditional lids.

Figure 18
From left: canning funnel, magnetic lid lifter, headspace tool / bubble popper, and jar lifter

Additional Tools

You will also need, at a minimum, a set of canning tools including a "bubble popper" / headspace tool and a jar lifter to get hot jars out of the canner. Optionally, you may want a canning funnel to aid in filling jars and a magnetic lid lifter to aid in picking up and positioning lids.

I have two additional tools I find very useful. The first is a simple block of wood that I use as a support under the jars when I carry them with the jar lifter from the stove to the location I cool my jars. I could, and originally did, use a potholder to do the job. However, I discovered the potholder got wet quickly and did not perform well across an entire canner full of jars. One day while unloading the canner I spied this small block of wood and used it instead to provide the extra support I wanted while transporting the jar. I was very pleased with the extra security it gave me over using just the jar lifter alone, and have kept it as a part of my tools ever since.

Figure 19
Supporting hot jar with small wood block

Figure 20
Wooden "Pickle Packer" works with regular (left) and wide-mouth (right) jars

The second tool is one I use, in particular, when canning tomatoes. Our first attempts at tomatoes resulted in about a half jar of tomatoes and a half jar of liquid after processing, even though the jar appeared completely full when we started. We figured there must be a better way and found it courtesy of a tool commonly referred to as a "Pickle Packer".

This simple tool, shown in Figure 20, is a solid block of acacia wood that has one end sized to fit into regular mouth jars (left) and the other sized to fit into wide mouth jars (right). It simply allows you to apply even pressure to the food in the jar, displacing air and, in the case of tomatoes, liquid from the center of the tomato. Using this tool allows you to pack many more tomatoes per jar. My husband is the master tomato packer. He fills the jar about 1/3 full and packs the tomatoes firmly into the jar with the "Pickle Packer". Next, he drains the excess liquid displaced by packing, leaving just the "meat" of the tomato. He repeats these steps until the jar is packed fully with tomatoes. Results will vary, but, typically, after he has used the "Pickle Packer" to load the jars, there is less than ½" of liquid in the bottom of the jar once the canning process is complete.

In addition to tomatoes and pickles, the "Pickle Packer" can be used for other vegetables such as shredded cabbage or fermented foods. The "Pickle Packer" can also be used as a muddler for crushing herbs, spices, and fruit.

Canning Methods

There are two canning methods: water bath and pressure. Which method you use depends on the type of food you are preserving. A few foods, such as tomatoes, can be canned via either method.

Water bath canning can only be used for high-acid foods such as:

- ▶ Tomatoes (with added acid)
- ▶ Fruits and fruit juices
- ▶ Jellies, jams, marmalades, butters, and preserves
- ▶ Pickles and relishes
- ▶ Salsas and chutneys

Pressure canning <u>must</u> be used for low-acid foods such as:

- ▶ Meats
- ▶ Vegetables
- ▶ Soups
- ▶ Tomatoes (without added acid)

I started my canning journey doing only water bath processing and worked my way up to pressure canning. I was nervous about using a pressure canner – remembering the horror stories of my youth. Inferior quality units built in the 40s and 50s were prone to developing clogged pressure regulators. With steam unable to vent, the pressure would build until finally something had to give – most often the lid – which went flying across the room. Redesigned in the 70s and 80s, modern pressure canners have never been safer, and grandma's tales of woe have been put to rest. As a result, I now very comfortably pressure can most of my foods. Water Bath Canning

Water Bath Canning

Figure 21
Water bath canner loaded with jars

The only additional tool you will need for water bath canning is a pot with a lid, deep enough to submerge your tallest jar by at least 1" with room left over for vigorous boiling. If you are also doing pressure canning, I recommend going ahead and using your pressure canner for your water bath canning as well. If you are just starting out and are not ready to invest in a pressure canner, a large stockpot will suffice. Some Instant Pots can also be used for water bath canning but should never be used for pressure canning, even though they are pressure devices.

In water bath canning, you are simply boiling the jars long enough to kill any microorganisms and to drive air out of the jar. Once all the air is out, a vacuum forms sealing the rubber gasket to the top of the jar, thus preventing any microbes from re-entering the sealed container. The length of time you need to boil depends on the food being canned and your elevation. "Why elevation?" you may ask. The higher the elevation, the lower the temperature at which water boils. Typical canning times given are for locations at 1000 feet above sea level or lower. Thus, if you live at a higher elevation, such as the 3430 feet shown on the iPhone Compass application in Figure 22, you will need to increase your processing time to ensure your foods are safely processed.

If you do not already know your elevation, you can determine it using a smartphone application such as Compass on an iPhone or any one of the many altimeter apps available for Android on the Google Play store. Alternatively, contact your local county extension agent to inquire about the appropriate adjustment for your area.

Figure 22
iPhone Compass app showing altitude (elevation)

Armed with your elevation you can find the required adjustments below:

❑ At 1,001 to 3,000 feet above sea level, increase processing time by 5 minutes.
❑ At 3,001 to 6,000 feet above sea level, increase processing time by 10 minutes.
❑ At 6,001 to 8,000 feet above sea level, increase processing time by 15 minutes.
❑ At 8,001 to 10,000 feet above sea level, increase processing time by 20 minutes.
❑ At more than 10,000 feet above sea level, increase processing time by 25 minutes.

It is important to note processing time does not start until the pot reaches a full boil. Maintain a full rolling boil with the lid on the pot for the required duration, reducing the heat, as needed, to prevent boil over. Once the required time has elapsed, remove the lid from the pot and allow the pot to cool for five minutes. Remove the jars using the jar lifter and place jars on a heat-proof surface in a location where they can remain undisturbed for 24 hours. I spread a towel on an out-of-the-way countertop to allow my jars to rest.

After 24 hours (and usually MUCH sooner), the "button" on a traditional jar lid should pop into a down position, indicating a good vacuum seal. You should be able to verify this by both visual inspection and by touch. If you do not have a good seal within 24 hours, refrigerate the jar and use within two weeks.

Figure 23
Button on modern canning lid, in concave position showing good seal

Pressure Canning

Pressure canning requires… you guessed it… a pressure canner. A pressure canner is different from a pressure cooker. While pressure cookers are designed to cook food fast, they are not designed to hold pressure and temperature in the same way a pressure canner is.

Modern pressure canners consist of a kettle with jar rack, lid with gasket, dial gauge, a vent/cover lock, a steam vent that can be closed to achieve varying pressures, and a safety fuse. The jar rack sits on the bottom of the canner and protects the jars from breakage under full boil. More importantly, modern pressure canners have inherent safety features to let steam escape, when necessary, to prevent over-pressurization.

With a pressure canner, it is not the pressure that renders the food in canning jars safe, but rather the very high heat obtained. As heat is applied, steam builds up and is trapped by the lid and gasket of the canner, increasing the pressure within the pot. As the pressure increases, so does the point at which water boils. At 15 pounds of pressure, water boils at 250 degrees – nearly 40 degrees higher than a non-pressurized pot. These high temperatures, when maintained for adequate duration, are capable of killing the microorganisms within the canning jars.

To be considered a pressure canner, the USDA requires the device to hold at least four quart jars, which translates to a canner size of 10-12 quarts. Canners come as large as 41 quarts, but unless you are an avid large-batch canner, the optimal size is in the 16-23 quart range. If your canner is too large, you will need to add empty jars to your batch to ensure your filled jars stay upright and you will use more energy to heat the additional water required by the larger size. Alternatively, if you have adequate storage space you could can water in those "spacer jars", rather than just using empty jars. Since I barely have enough room for all my home canned foods, I elect to use empty jars as spacers for both pressure and water bath canning

Figure 24
Modern 23-quart pressure canner

as you see in the photo in Figure 21. I find a 23-quart canner to be perfect for my needs, providing the right balance between size and energy requirements.

The number of jars you can run per batch will depend on the size of your canner and the size of the jars you are processing. When processing quarts in the typical 23-quart canner, you can process seven jars – six around the outside plus one in the middle. Seven wide-mouth pints can also be processed in the same configuration. However, if your pints are all standard mouth, you will be able to place at least one, and possibly two more, on a single layer in the canner. If you have more than seven pints to process, you can also double stack the jars, using a jar rack in between the layers. By double stacking, as many as 16 pint jars can be processed in a single load. With the smaller half or quarter pint jars, a 23-quart canner can handle as many as 22 jars when double stacked!

To pressure can, place the jar rack in the bottom of the pot and add two to three inches of water, more if advised by the manufacturer or by a specific canning recipe. Unlike water bath canning, you do not need to cover the jars with water. In pressure canning, the smaller volume of water is used to create steam, which, in a closed canner, creates pressure. Add the jars, double stacking if desired, with a second jar rack between layers. If the jars to be processed do not fully fill the space in your canner, add water filled "spacer" jars, as needed, to keep all jars upright for the duration of the canning cycle.

Figure 25
Pressure gauge on modern canner

Ensure the canner lid gasket seats properly in the lid. Place the lid on the canner and secure by either rotating the lid or locking the clamps, depending on the style of canner you are using.

Apply high heat to achieve boiling. Once the canner has reached boiling, reduce the heat to a level that maintains a solid boil, but reduces the chance of glass breakage.

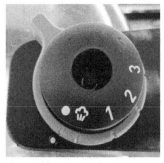

Before pressurizing the canner, it is important to make sure there is no air trapped inside the closed canner. This safety measure is accomplished through the venting process, which releases steam from the canner, and with it, eliminates the potential for trapped air. The mechanism used to vent a canner will vary. On the canner pressure dial shown in Figure 26, the small dot indicates the current setting on the canner. Venting will occur when the small dot is aligned with either the large dot (where this canner is currently set), or the vent position next to the large dot, represented by the steam image. On this canner, steam is released through the opening in the middle of the pressure dial. By contrast,

Figure 26
Dial for adjusting and venting pressure on pressure canner

some canners will have a fixed vent, onto which a weight is placed to pressurize the canner as shown in Figure 27. Regardless of the type of canner, while venting, pressure does not build up inside the canner. Allow the canner to vent for ten minutes before beginning to pressurize the canner.

As with water bath canning, in pressure canning, it is also necessary to make adjustments based on your elevation. While with boiling water canning you adjust the length of time the food is processed in the boiling water, with pressure canning you must adjust the pounds of pressure under which the food is processed. The way the adjustment is made will vary slightly based on your type of canner.

Figure 27
Weighted pressure relief valve

On the canner pictured in Figure 26, which has a dial gauge, rotating the dial to the number one position will achieve approximately five pounds of pressure, to number two will achieve approximately ten pounds of pressure, and to number three will achieve approximately fifteen pounds of pressure. Adjusting the amount of heat applied to the canner will provide fine-tuning of the pressure above or below these increments. Different canners will have different methods for adjusting pressure.

The chart below provides the amount of pressure to use based on the elevation3. Refer to the information under water bath canning earlier in this chapter for ways to determine your altitude.

Altitude (Elevation) (feet above sea level)	Weighted Gauge (pounds of pressure)	Dial-Gauge (pounds of pressure)
0-1000	10	11
1001 – 2000	15	11
2001 - 3000	15	12
3001 - 6000	15	13
6001 - 8000	15	14
8001 +	15	15

References

1. Suzanne Waring, "Canning – On the Ball? Do You Kerr? It's All Straight from the Jarden", Idaho Senior Independent, October 5, 2020, https://www.idahoseniorindependent.com/canning/.

2. "How to Reuse Canning Lids", A Traditional Life Blog, accessed September 14, 2021, https://atraditionallife.com/how-to-reuse-canning-lids/.

3. Megan Erickson, "Altitude Adjustments for Home Canning", South Dakota State University Extension, September 11, 2020, https://extension.sdstate.edu/altitude-adjustments-home-canning.

"You are to take every kind of food that is to be eaten and store it away as food for you and for them."

- Genesis 6:21

Chapter 8
Canning Tips and Resources

One of the great things about canning is you can start out small and inexpensive, then expand the range of your canning as your experience grows. Jams and preserves make a great first project with the only tools required being a few quarter or half pint canning jars, lids and rings, and a pot big enough to hold the jars and cover them by at least one inch of water. A set of basic canning tools (jar lifter and bubble remover being paramount) can be purchased for $15 or less.

I started my canning journey with just a few jars of blackberry jam, followed soon after by peach preserves and sliced peaches. Not knowing any better, I slowly peeled a whole basket of slippery peaches by hand for those first peach experiments. Shortly after, I discovered there is a much easier way to peel peaches! Cut a shallow X in the bottom of the peach (opposite the stem), then place in boiling water for approximately 1 minute, then plunge into an ice bath (cold water further chilled with plenty of ice cubes). The skins will loosen and practically fall off the peach. The important bonus of this method is that none of the meat of the peach is lost the way it was when I hand-peeled them.

Great Choices for Canning

▶ Jams and Jellies

▶ Tomatoes

▶ Sweet Potatoes

▶ Peaches

▶ Apples and Applesauce

▶ Chicken

▶ Beef

From fruits, I moved on to tomatoes – still technically a fruit, but treated like a vegetable. In fact, you can peel tomatoes the same way you peel peaches. Given my husband's Sicilian heritage, in our house, tomatoes are a staple. Tomatoes are one of the few foods where you have the option of processing by either water bath or pressure canning methods. Early in my canning journey, I opted for water bath canning, although to process the quarts we needed it was time to acquire a taller pot. It is very important to be able to cover your jars by at least 1" of water at all times when water bath canning. Be sure to watch for evaporation or boil over during the canning process, and add water, if necessary, to maintain that 1" minimum

After a couple successful seasons of water bath canning, I felt ready to expand my range of foods with pressure canning. I recommend purchasing a pressure canner only from a well-recognized manufacturer such as Presto or All-American, rather than taking a chance with your dear old grandmother's canner that may not be equipped with today's modern safety features. Those aforementioned horror stories about pressure cookers definitely slowed my transition from water bath to pressure canning unnecessarily. Equipped with a 23-quart Presto canner, I pressure canned the next season's tomatoes.

Once comfortable with the idea of pressure canning, my canning pursuits broadened significantly. Potatoes, sweet potatoes, and applesauce soon followed. At a regional preparedness conference, I learned to can meats and added chicken, beef and bacon to my inventory.

MY TOP 5 CANNING TIPS

▶ **Use only Ball or Kerr lids**

▶ **Do not reuse lids for canning, except Tattler Reusable Canning Lids**

▶ **Check jars and lids for imperfections before use / reuse**

▶ **Consider standardizing on either wide or regular mouth jars**

▶ **Use a jar packer (aka "pickle packer") to maximize jar fill**

Grid-down Canning

The term, "grid-down", refers to an absence of electrical power – the power "grid" is down and not expected to be operational any time soon. Grid-down is more than just a power outage. Perhaps the single best thing about canning is the fact that having electricity is not an absolute requirement. Therefore, the process for grid-down canning remains essentially unchanged from traditional canning.

If you have a gas stove, no alterations are necessary, except for the fact that you may need to light the stove manually. Those with an electric stove will need to use an alternate heat source. A side burner on a gas grill can be a great choice. A camp stove could also work. If all else fails, canning can be accomplished over an open fire. With any alternative heat source, you are likely to find temperature regulation more difficult. You will need to keep a much closer eye on the pot throughout the process, as maintaining temperature and pressure is essential to successful canning.

In an extended grid-down scenario, or alternatively, a product shortage – as experienced by many during the COVID-19 pandemic – availability of new canning lids may be severely limited or even non-existent. If forced to reuse lids, inspect each lid very carefully before using and check the seal on each jar both 24 hours after canning and monthly thereafter. Even if the lid seals initially, experience has shown that seals on re-used lids are likely to fail faster than new lids. Consider keeping reusable Tattler lids and seals on hand to supplement. A set of replacement rubber seals for your Tattler lids is also a good idea. I also recommend keeping at least one to two dozen extra quart jars on hand at all times. In an extended grid-down scenario – and particularly if you do not have a generator – you should begin canning the frozen foods in your freezer within 24-36 hours in order to preserve as much of the food as possible.

Canning Resources

Because of the inherent risk of botulism from faulty canning, it is important to use only tested recipes from a reliable source.

By far my favorite canning book is the *Ball Complete Book of Home Preserving,* edited by Judi Kingry and Lauren Devine. This hardcover resource is available from Amazon or from your local emergency preparedness store.

Figure 28
Two of my favorite resources on home canning, from Ball and from the US Department of Agriculture

With over 400 recipes, this book provides basic canning recipes for fruits, vegetables, and meats plus many creative variations including relishes and chutneys, marmalades, and more, all from the most trusted name in canning.

Another solid resource is *The Complete Book of Home Canning* produced by the U.S. Department of Agriculture, another trusted font of canning information.

This valuable resource includes sections on fermented foods, including pickled foods for special diets and reduced-sugar fruit spreads. The section on poultry, red meats, and seafood includes instructions for clams, oysters, crab, and fish.

Each of these books are available for $20 or less, but you do not have to buy a book to gain access to excellent resources on canning.

The National Center for Home Food Preservation (NCHFP), based at the University of Georgia, has an excellent free website, found at https://nchfp.uga.edu/can_home. html. In addition to the standard processing information on fruits, vegetables, and meats, the NCHFP site also includes a section on salsa as well as a section on nuts and nut products.

Other great free resources include:

- **Information sheets from North Carolina State University on canning safely, troubleshooting problems, and reprocessing home canned foods** *https://foodsafety.ces.ncsu.edu/general-canning*

- **Home Canning for Beginners, which includes a webinar** *https://mecklenburg.ces.ncsu.edu/canit*

Chapter 9
Canning Step-by-step

This chapter provides a step-by-step reference guide to canning. Steps 1-20 are the same regardless of which method you are using, with minor exceptions on step 6 and 13 called out in *italics for water bath canning* and in **bold for pressure canning**.

- *For water bath canning, continue with steps 21 – 34.*
- **For pressure canning, skip forward to steps 35 – 49.**

1. Determine the size and number of jars required for the volume of food you plan to preserve. Add 1-2 more just in case your estimate is a little off.

2. Gather jars and inspect carefully for any signs of damage. This might include cracks in the jar or subtle chips that might have formed on the lip of the jar. I recommend running your finger gently over the lip as these defects can be hard to see but can often be felt. *Be careful, to avoid cuts!*

3. Gather the correct size (regular or wide-mouth) rings and a corresponding <u>NEW</u> lid for each jar. Remember to reuse lids ONLY in an emergency or if they are specifically designed for that purpose (e.g. Tattler lids). Discard any dented, damaged, or corroded rings.

4. Hand wash all jars, lids, and rings and place on a clean towel to drain. Do not sterilize lids and rings in a dishwasher as this may damage the rubber seal or corrode the ring. They do not need to be dried.

5. While the actual canning process will, in most cases, kill any bacteria inside the jar, all jars should be sterilized prior to use, as the processing time for some foods is <u>not</u> sufficient to ensure all microorganisms are killed. Do not take a chance. Sterilize your jars either by washing the dishwasher or by hand washing and boiling for no less than 10 minutes.

6. Filling a cold jar with hot contents or introducing a cold jar to a hot pot can cause the jar to crack or even shatter. Additionally, submerging a jar (especially an empty jar) in hot water can cause splattering and burns. Thus, it is necessary to make sure jars are preheated prior to filling. If you are sterilizing your jars in the dishwasher, you can keep the jars warm by leaving the dishwasher closed until you are ready to use the jars.

   Otherwise, if you are water bath canning, place the jar rack into the bottom of the canner (recommended, but not required) and then add empty jars, without lids or rings, into the canner. Add water, filling the jars and bringing the water level to about just above the top of the jars. Bring the water to a simmer to heat but not boil the jars. You will simply add your filled jars back to this already warmed water (step 18) to start the canning process.

If you are pressure canning, fill a separate large pot with water to a level that will just cover the jars. Add empty jars, without lids or rings to this pot. Bring the water to a simmer to heat but not boil the jars. In addition, place 2-3" of water into the canner but do not apply heat yet.

7. OPTIONAL: Place lids into a small saucepan and cover with water. Simmer on low heat. The idea here is simply to warm the rubber on the lids to aid in forming a good seal. Recently, the USDA has updated their guidance to say this step is no longer necessary, but many canners, including myself, still perform this step.

8. Set the rings aside.

9. Follow the recipe to prepare the food you wish to can.

10. Using the jar lifter, remove one jar from the hot water bath, carefully emptying the water from the jar back into the pot.

11. Place the hot jar on a heat-safe surface, not only to protect the surface, but also to protect the jar from breakage due to temperature shock.

12. Place the jar-filling funnel in the top of the jar, if desired. As I have become more experienced as a canner, I have found myself using the funnel less and less. A deep spoon or ladle may be used instead.

13. Ladle the prepared food into the jars, leaving the amount of headspace indicated in the recipe and as required by the canning method. Headspace is the empty space between the top of the jar and the top of the food and is required because foods will expand during the canning process. Failing to leave the right amount of headspace can result in failures to seal and food leakage during the canning process.

    Water bath canning: Most foods require ½" headspace. Jams, jellies, and preserves require ¼" headspace. **Pressure canning: Headspace should be 1".**

    Use the headspace tool, marked with ¼", ½", and 1" depths, to measure your headspace. Adjust by adding or removing small amounts of food or canning liquid as necessary until the required level is achieved.

14. Turn the headspace tool 180 degrees (reverse) to use the other end of this tool to aid in removal of bubbles. If you do not have a headspace tool, use a thin non-metal spatula or a chopstick. Run the tool around the inside of the jar, between the food and the glass to remove bubbles. I like to start at the rim and push down to the bottom of the jar then back up. I repeat this, moving around the jar in small, over-

lapping increments, turning the jar as I go, until I have gone all the way around the jar. Repeat, if desired.

15. Use a paper towel or small clean cloth to wipe all the way around the rim of the jar. This is a critical step to remove any debris on the lip of the jar, as this will cause a failure to seal. If canning meats, moisten the cloth with a little bit of white vinegar before wiping.

16. Use the magnetic lid lifter tool or non-metal tongs to remove one lid from the water bath, if used, and place on the jar. If a water bath was not used, simply place one of the lids you have set aside on the jar, centering to ensure the lid covers the entire top of the jar.

17. Place one of the rings you have set aside on the jar, keeping one finger on the lid to insure it stays in place. Screw the lid onto the jar until resistance is met and then increase until finger-tight. If using reusable lids, follow the directions provided with the lids to tighten correctly. Do not over-tighten the rings as this can result in seal failure during the canning process.

18. Place the filled and sealed jar back into the canner, adjusting the placement of other jars, if necessary.

19. Repeat the process until all jars are filled. If you have a jar that is less than full, place the jar in the refrigerator and use within 1-2 weeks, depending on the type of food.

20. Once all the filled jars have been returned to the canner (using two layers if applicable), add empty (water-filled) jars as needed to maintain spacing. These extra empty jars ensure filled jars do not overturn while boiling.

Water Bath Canning

21. Add or subtract water as required to cover the jars by at least 1".

22. Place the lid on the canner.

23. Bring the canner to a full-rolling boil using high heat.

24. Reduce the heat but maintain boil. Avoid boiling too energetically or jar breakage could occur.

25. Boil for the length of time specified in your recipe, adjusting for your altitude if required (see Chapter 7). Do not start timing until the water has reached a sustained, full boil.

26. Once the required time has expired, turn off the heat and remove the lid.

27. Allow the canner to rest for 10 minutes.

28. Spread a dishtowel or other cloth in a heat-safe location where the jars can remain undisturbed.

29. Using the jar lifter, remove the jars one at a time and place them on the towel. I use a small block of wood to support the jar as I carry it from stove to counter, just for peace of mind.

30. Allow the jars to rest undisturbed for 24 hours.

31. After 24 hours, inspect all jars to verify a good seal formed on each. This can be ascertained by looking at and feeling the "button" on the top of each lid and verifying this area is concave (bows down into the jar) rather than convex (bows up away from the jar). If any jars are found to have a convex button, the seal is compromised, and the jar should be placed in the refrigerator and used within 1-2 weeks.

32. Wipe down all jars with a warm cloth, using soap, if required, to remove any residue adhered to the jar.

33. Remove the ring. Storing without the ring is actually the best practice, as once the seal has formed the ring is no longer needed. However, if you choose to store with the ring in place, clean the ring thoroughly, then replace before storing.

34. Label all jars with contents and date processed. Jars should be stored in as cool a location as possible (not freezing!) and away from light to ensure they remain fresh as long as possible.

Pressure Canning

35. Adjust the water level as recommended for your specific canner. I recommend keeping your canner's user guide with your canning recipes for ready reference.

36. Place the lid on your canner and lock the lid as directed for your canner. If using a canner with a weight, leave it off at this time or leave the canner in the vent position.

37. Bring the water to a boil over medium-high heat. When steam starts coming from the vent, the water is boiling.

38. Adjust the heat to maintain a steady (but not vigorous) boil and allow steam to vent for 10 minutes.

39. Place the weight on the canner or set the dial to apply pressure per your canner's instructions, adjusting for altitude as required (see Chapter 7).

40. Monitor the pressure and begin timing only once the pressure required by your recipe has been achieved.

41. Once the processing time has elapsed, turn off the heat and allow the pressure to reduce to zero. The safety lock will not allow the lid to be removed while the canner is still under pressure. DO NOT force-cool the canner. Allow it to cool naturally.

42. Once the canner has cooled and the safety lock has released, remove the lid and allow the canner to rest for 10 minutes.

43. Spread a dishtowel or other cloth in a heat safe location where the jars can remain undisturbed.

44. Using the jar lifter, remove the jars one at a time and place them on the towel. I use a small block of wood to support the jar as I carry it from stove to counter, just for peace of mind.

45. Allow the jar to rest undisturbed for 24 hours.

46. After 24 hours, inspect all jars to verify a good seal formed on each. This can be ascertained by looking at and feeling the "button" on the top of each lid and verifying this area is concave (bows down into the jar) rather than convex (bows up away from the jar). If any jars are found to have a convex button, the seal is compromised, and the jar should be placed in the refrigerator and used within 1-2 weeks.

47. Wipe down all jars with a warm cloth, using soap if required to remove any residue that is adhered to the jar.

48. Remove the ring. Storing without the ring is actually the best practice, as once the seal has formed the ring is no longer needed. However, if you choose to store with the ring in place, clean the ring thoroughly, then replace before storing.

49. Label all jars with contents and date processed. Jars should be stored in as cool a location as possible (not freezing!) and away from light to ensure they remain fresh as long as possible.

> *"The average person is still under the aberrant delusion that food should be somebody else's responsibility until I'm ready to eat it."*
> **- Joel Salatin**

 # Chapter 10
Favorite Canning Recipes

Building Food Security is not intended to be a recipe book, but I will share a few of my favorite recipes - ones that have helped me advance my knowledge of canning. Refer to Chapter 9 for full details on preparing jars, lids, and rings, as well as directions for filling jars and processing based on the method(s) indicated in the recipe.

You will notice all the fruit recipes are sugar free, showcasing the natural sweetness of the fruit. When preparing jams, I use a low or no sugar pectin and add a little Splenda, which is recognized as the most stable alternative sweetener when heated. If you prefer to use sugar, refer to the recipe on the regular pectin box for the correct amount of sugar to use.

Sugar Free Peach Jam

Makes approximately 8 pints

»   3 pounds fresh peaches, finely chopped to make 3 cups
»   ¾ cup water
»   1 box Sure-Jell for Less or No Sugar Needed Recipes Fruit Pectin
»   ½ cup Splenda No Calorie Sweetener or 12 Splenda Packets
»   Optional: ¼ teaspoon butter (reduces foaming)

Place chopped fruit into a saucepan. Add ¾ cup water and fruit pectin. Stir. Add butter, if using. Bring mixture to a full rolling boil (a boil that does not stop when stirred). Remove from heat. Stir in Splenda. Skim off any foam. Ladle into jars, leaving ¼" headspace. Process using water bath method for 10 minutes, adjusting for altitude.

Sugar Free Berry Jam

Makes approximately 6 pints

»   2 quarts blackberries or strawberries
»   1 cup water
»   4 ½ Tablespoons Sure-Jell for Less or No Sugar Needed Recipes Fruit Pectin
»   Up to 1 ½ cups Splenda No Calorie Sweetener
»   Optional: ¼ teaspoon butter (reduces foaming)

Crush berries, a few at a time, with a potato masher. Add 1 cup water and fruit pectin. Stir. Add butter, if using. Bring mixture to a full rolling boil (a boil that does not stop when stirred). Remove from heat. Stir in Splenda. Skim off any foam. Ladle into jar leaving ¼" headspace. Process using water bath method for 10 minutes, adjusting for altitude.

Sugar Free Applesauce

Makes approximately 8 pints

»   12 pounds of apples (Fuji recommended)
»   6 tablespoons lemon juice, divided
»   Optional: ½ cup Splenda No Calorie Sweetener or 12 Splenda Packets (I do not add Splenda)
»   Water

Place 2 cups of cold water in a bowl and add 2 tablespoons lemon juice. Peel and slice apples, placing into prepared lemon water immediately for 3-5 minutes to prevent browning. Drain. Place apples in a large stainless steel saucepan or stockpot. Add just enough water to cover apples. Bring to a boil over medium-high heat, stirring regularly to prevent sticking. Reduce heat and continue boiling until tender. (Note: time will vary from 5-20 minutes depending on type of apple, ripeness, and how thickly sliced).

Remove from heat and allow to cool slightly. Puree the cooked apples in batches, using a food processor or blender, until desired smoothness reached. (I prefer to leave mine slightly chunky). Return pureed apples to saucepan. Add Splenda (or sugar), if using. Add remainder of lemon juice. Bring to a low boil and continue to boil while filling jars to avoid premature thickening.

Ladle into jars, leaving ½" headspace. Process using water bath method for 20 minutes.

Sugar Free Sliced Apples (pictured on cover)

Makes approximately 8 pints

»   12 pounds apples (Fuji recommended)
»   7 cups water, divided
»   ½ cup Splenda No Calorie Sweetener or 12 Splenda Packets
»   2 Tablespoons lemon juice

Place 2 cups of cold water in a bowl and add 2 tablespoons lemon juice. Peel and slice apples, placing into prepared lemon water immediately for 3-5 minutes to prevent browning.

Prepare ultra-light sugar free syrup by dissolving ½ cup Splenda in 5 cups water in a large stainless steel saucepan or stockpot. Drain lemon water from apples and add apples to ultra-light syrup. Bring to a boil over medium-high heat. Reduce heat and continue to boil for 5 minutes.

Pack apples into jar leaving ½" headspace. Process using water bath method for 20 minutes.

Sugar Free Sliced Peaches

Makes approximately 8 pints

- » 8 to 12 pounds peaches
- » 7 cups water, divided
- » ½ cup Splenda
- » 2 Tablespoons lemon juice

Place 2 cups of cold water in a bowl and add 2 tablespoons lemon juice. In another large bowl, add cold water and ice cubes to make an ice bath. Cut an X on the bottom of each peach and place in boiling water for 1 minute to loosen skin. Remove from heat and place into prepared ice bath. Skin will slip off easily. Pit and slice peaches, placing into prepared lemon water immediately for 3-5 minutes to prevent browning.

Prepare ultra-light sugar free syrup by dissolving ½ cup Splenda in 5 cups water in a large stainless steel saucepan or stockpot. Drain lemon water from peaches and add peaches to ultra-light syrup. Bring to a boil over medium-high heat. Reduce heat and continue to boil for 5 minutes.

Pack peaches into jar leaving ½" headspace. Process using water bath method for 25 minutes.

Note: Two pints of apples or peaches are perfect for making a low/no sugar pie! If desired, package in quarts for pies, processing for 30 minutes instead of 25.

White Potatoes

Makes 4 quarts

- » 12 pounds small to medium white potatoes
- » Water

Wash and peel potatoes. Wash again. Small potatoes may be left whole. Cut larger potatoes into small cubes. Place into stainless steel saucepan or stockpot filled with cold water immediately to prevent browning.

Bring to a boil over medium-heat. Boil small cubes 2 minutes and whole potatoes or larger cubes 10 minutes, heating through but keeping potatoes firm.

Drain. Pack potatoes into hot jars. Add fresh boiling water to cover potatoes, leaving ½" headspace. Process quarts for 40 minutes or pints for 35 minutes.

Tomatoes (Whole, Halved, or Quartered)

Makes 4 quarts or 8 pints

» Approximately 32 Roma tomatoes or equivalent canning tomatoes
» Citric Acid or lemon juice
» Water

In a large bowl, add cold water and ice cubes to make an ice bath. Core and cut an X on the bottom of each tomato. Place in boiling water for 3 minutes to loosen skin. Remove from boiling water and place into ice bath. Slip skins from tomato. Halve or quarter, if desired.

Add a few tomatoes. Pack very firmly with a pickle packer. Drain excess liquid. Add more tomatoes and repeat as required to fill jar. Add ½ teaspoon citric acid for quarts (¼ teaspoon for pints) or 2 Tablespoons lemon juice for quarts (1 Tablespoon for pints). Add the minimum amount of tomato juice or water, if required, to achieve 1" headspace for pressure canning or ½" for water bath. Ideally, adjust your headspace with tomatoes only, adding no extra liquid.

Water bath: Process for 45 minutes for quarts or 40 minutes for pints, adjusting for altitude as shown in the water bath altitude adjustment chart in Chapter 7.

Pressure canning: Process at 10 pounds pressure for 25 minutes, adjusting pressure to altitude and canner type as shown in the pressure canning altitude adjustment chart in Chapter 7.

Chicken

Makes 4 quarts or 8 pints

» 8 large boneless, skinless chicken breasts
» Water or low-fat chicken broth

Cut chicken breasts into 1" cubes. Drop raw chicken into jars, packing only lightly to ensure chicken will cook thoroughly. Fill jar with boiling water or low-fat broth, leaving 1" headspace. Wipe rim with paper towel moistened with vinegar to remove any meat juices. Process in pressure canner at 10 pounds of pressure, adjusted for altitude and canner type (see Chapter 7) for 65 minutes for pints or 90 minutes for quarts.

Beef, Lamb, Venison, Pork, or Veal (Chunks)

Makes 4 quarts or 8 pints

»   Approximately 8 pounds of beef, venison, pork, or veal
»   Water

Cut meat into 1" chunks, trimming as much fat as possible. Drop raw meat into jars, packing only lightly to ensure meat will cook thoroughly. Fill jar with boiling water, leaving 1" headspace. Wipe rim with paper towel moistened with vinegar to remove any meat juices. Process in pressure canner at 10 pounds of pressure, adjusted for altitude and canner type (see Chapter 7) for 75 minutes for pints and 90 minutes for quarts.

Ground Beef, Lamb, Venison, Pork, or Veal

Makes 4 quarts or 8 pints

»   Approximately 8 pounds of ground beef, lamb, venison, pork, or veal
»   Water or low-fat broth

Brown ground meat in skillet and drain excess fat. (Optional: Rinse with warm water to remove additional fat.) Add 1 to 1 ½ cups of water or low-fat broth to drained beef. Ladle into jars, leaving 1" headspace. Wipe rim with paper towel moistened with vinegar to remove any meat juices. Process in pressure canner at 10 pounds of pressure, adjusted for altitude and canner type (see Chapter 7) for 75 minutes for pints and 90 minutes for quarts.

> *"By failing to prepare you are preparing to fail."*
> - Benjamin Franklin

PART THREE
Dehydrating

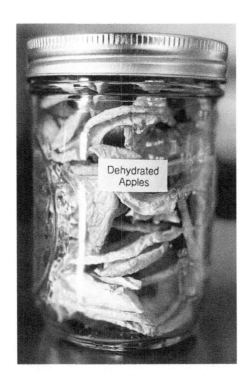

Chapter 11
What is Dehydrating?

Dehydrating is the process of evaporating moisture through the application of heat to reduce the moisture content of food to a level at which it can remain shelf stable. By removing enough moisture, bacteria, yeast, and molds cannot grow.

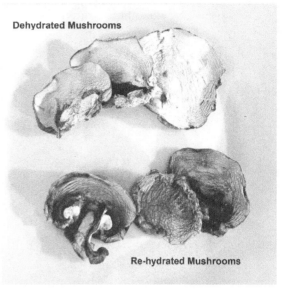

Dehydrated Mushrooms

Re-hydrated Mushrooms

Figure 29
Comparison of dehydrated and rehydrated mushrooms

Dehydrating creates a very compact, lightweight food store, since most of the weight in food derives from moisture. This also means there are more calories by weight. One ounce of dehydrated apple, for example, has approximately 75 calories, five times more than the calories in one ounce of fresh apple slices. In addition, the dehydration process destroys vitamins A and C. B vitamins are also reduced, so it is necessary to get these vitamins from other sources rather than relying solely on dehydrated foods.

Dehydrating requires low humidity, a source of low heat, and, ideally, air circulation. The amount of heat required varies based on the type of food dehydrated. Herbs need only a temperature of 110 degrees. Meats, on the other hand, require higher temperatures – typically around 145 to 155 degrees – and faster drying times, to be safely dehydrated. The heat warms but does not cook the foods. However, dehydrated foods typically cook faster than their fresh counterparts, when used in later food preparation.

Dehydrating likely has been around as long as man, but the first references to dehydrating appear about 12,000 BC in the Middle East and Orient. Egyptians were known to be dehydrating by 2800 BC. [1]

While some dehydration methods require electricity, the low heat required to dry the food items may be supplied by either natural or artificial means. We will talk more about the various methods of dehydrating in the next section.

Dehydrated foods can be consumed in their dried form, or moisture can be reintroduced to return the food to a state similar to the original. This process is referred to as rehydration. Some foods rehydrate better than others do. Seldom will a food rehydrate to the exact same consistency as the original. Store dehydrated food items away from moisture or the rehydration process will begin prematurely, allowing bacteria, yeast, and mold to grow.

References

1. Brian A. Nummer, "Historical Origins of Food Preservation", National Center for Home Food Preservation, May 2002, https://nchfp.uga.edu/publications/nchfp/factsheets/food_pres_hist.html.

Chapter 12
Dehydrating Tools and Methods

Want to get started in dehydrating? First, think about what types of food you plan to dry, as this may influence your choice of method. Your method selection will dictate your tools.

If costs are a concern, consider air, sun, or oven dehydrating.

- Air dehydrating has limited uses, but is a good choice for herbs, peppers, onions, and mushrooms.
- Sun dehydrating is a wise choice if you want to use the same method grid up or grid down, but is only useful for fruits (including tomatoes) and beans. Sun drying of meats and other vegetables is not recommended, although there are some individuals who do.
- Oven dehydrating will only work off grid if you have a gas stove you can light without electricity, or while you have the use of a generator. However, you can use oven dehydrating for fruits, vegetables, and meats.
- If you prefer a dedicated and more easily controlled environment for your dehydrating, choose one of the many stand-alone dehydrators on the market.

Dehydrating Methods

Air Dehydrating

Air dehydrating is the simplest, but most limited technique, being useful only for herbs, hot peppers, onions, shallots, garlic, and mushrooms. Air dehydrating differs from sun dehydrating in that it is typically done indoors with the items enclosed in a paper bag, tied in small bunches, or in the case of onions, shallots and garlic, fashioned into braids. The bag, bunch, or braid is suspended in an area where it can remain undisturbed until dry, such as in an attic, spare bedroom, or screen enclosed porch.

An inexpensive, albeit limited option, the only tools required for air dehydrating are a paper bag of suitable size (if using) and kitchen twine to tie and suspend the food to be dried.

Figure 30
Air dehydrated onion braid

Sun Dehydrating

A good friend of mine relies exclusively on sun hydrating and has for many years. The biggest challenges with this method are the length of time required and the need to manage moisture and pests closely.

Sun dehydrating uses the radiant heat of the sun along with wind, if present. A minimum temperature of 85 degrees is recommended for sun dehydrating, but is not absolutely essential. Humidity is also a factor, with humidity below 60% preferred. Of the two, humidity is a bigger concern than temperature.

Clearly, foods will dry faster on hotter days and in hotter climates, but there is a trick that can help amplify the temperatures and at the same time provide moisture and pest control. By placing the items to dry on the dashboard of a vehicle, you can use the windshield to magnify the heat.

With limited exceptions, sun dehydrating will take multiple days to complete and, as a result, it will be necessary to protect the drying items from rain and dew each day. Typically, this means bringing the drying foodstuffs in before the sun goes down each day, and putting them out again the next morning. This may need to be repeated for three to five days, or more.

Figure 31
Sun drying tomatoes on wire frames

The simplest approach is to spread the items to be dried on a clean cloth (like an old bedsheet). The downside of using a piece of cloth is that it is difficult to move the foodstuffs quickly. While a cloth can be gathered up and lifted with the food items still on it, the foods will have to be spread out again when the sheets are laid out again the next day. Drying may be slowed if pieces with more moisture are in contact with pieces with less moisture overnight.

To overcome this, stretch the cloth around a simple frame made with furring strips or other surplus wood. This will enable you pick up and move the entire drying rack with little impact on the items laid out on the cloth. Screening can be substituted for cloth and similarly attached to a frame. Avoid using hardware cloth, which is typically galvanized and can impart harmful residue into the food as it dries. Frames can be stacked overnight, minimizing the amount of space required to store them.

If you plan to use the dashboard method for some or all of your drying, you will need to take that into consideration when planning the size of your drying frames. The added advantage of dashboard drying is it provides protection from rain and dew as well as most pests. The downside is the limited amount of space, even if you have front and rear windows available. Windows should be left down, if possible, to allow for air movement which aids in drying.

Fruits are ideally suited for sun dehydrating. Use extreme caution when dehydrating vegetables and inspect daily for mold. Discard at the first sign of mold growth. Meats should <u>never</u> be sun dehydrated, as the extended drying times encourage bacterial growth.

Wash, pit, and/or cut food items to the desired size. Keep in mind that thick or chunky pieces will take longer to dry. Place your cloth or frame in full sun on a concrete, reflective, or metal backing to help maintain even heating. Spread the food items on your cloth or frame in a single layer, with space around each piece for airflow. Pieces that touch will slow drying, particularly with high moisture or very dense foods. If insects are a problem, consider covering the food items with netting or cheesecloth. Turn the food items at least once per day with a spatula or by hand.

Bring in the food items nightly to avoid condensation and always keep an eye out for precipitation while drying. Repeat the process daily for three to four days, more if required, to achieve full dryness. Test the foods daily, beginning on day three. Vegetables should be brittle and snap when flexed. Fruits should be almost brittle.

Oven Dehydrating

Oven dehydrating eliminates some of the issues of sun dehydrating while remaining an option in a grid-down (long-term power outage) situation so long as you can light the oven manually, or if a generator is available to power the stove. However, consider the amount of fuel that will be required when using this method during an extended grid-down situation. It may still be the best option if it means being able to preserve the foods in your freezer before they spoil, if the power will not be coming back on soon.

Oven dehydrating provides a pest and moisture free environment for drying fruits, vegetables, and meats. It is faster than sun dehydrating but typically takes longer than commercial dehydrators due to the lack of air circulation. Convection ovens overcome this limitation and should provide drying times similar to that of commercial dehydrators. The biggest drawback for oven dehydrating is the amount of space available, as most ovens have only two racks, requiring you to do smaller batches more frequently. As a result commercial dehydrators will typically be much more energy efficient. If you plan to do a lot of oven dehydrating, look at used appliance stores for extra oven racks you can use to double your dehydrating capacity, as most ovens do have three to four rack positions available on which you can place the extra racks.

Make sure the oven is capable of a 140°F or a 'Keep Warm' setting. Temperatures higher than 140 degrees will result in the food cooking before it can dry.

Oven dehydrating can be done year-round and does not have the temperature and humidity limitations of sun dehydrating. However, keep in mind that a running oven will increase the ambient temperature of the room since, unless you are using a convection oven, the oven door should be propped open while dehydrating. While useful in the winter perhaps, adding three to five degrees to the room temperature in Florida in August may be less than desirable.

Figure 32
Oven door left ajar for air circulation for oven dehydrating

Items to be dried are placed on cookie sheets or other oven safe containers. The lower the sides on the container, the better the air circulation. To improve air circulation on a non-convection oven, consider placing a fan near the open oven door to add some air movement. Place an oven thermometer near the foods to monitor the actual temperature.

Turn foods with a spatula every four hours. Check food for dryness after eight hours if your oven has airflow (convection or fan produced) or after ten hours if no airflow is available. As with sun dehydrating, foods are done when vegetables are brittle and fruits are nearly brittle. Avoid the temptation to turn up the heat on the oven, as this will result in the outside becoming dry while the interior still contains moisture, which will cause mold to form when stored.

Dehydrating with a commercial dehydrator

There are dozens of dehydrators on the market, ranging in price from $50 - $700. Important features to look for when choosing a dehydrator include a temperature control which can be adjusted from at least 110 - 160°F, a timer which can run up to 24 hours, good airflow throughout the unit, sufficient space for your desired volume of dehydrating, and expandability to increase dehydrating volume in the future.

Dehydrators come in two configurations: stackable trays and slide-in, with stackable being the most common format. The advantage of stackable trays is you can use as few or as many as you need, subject to the limits of the particular device. With a slide-in configuration, you are limited to a fixed amount of space, holding a fixed number of racks.

My first dehydrator – actually my husband's dehydrator – was round with five stackable trays. He had purchased it to make jerky with his kids. I found the round configuration limited what I could fit on the rack, so when I was ready to expand, I decided to look for a rectangular unit.

On the high end of the dehydrator spectrum is the Excalibur 9-tray slide-in unit, which retails for anywhere from $250 - $370 depending on the exact configuration. A 4-rack version is also available.

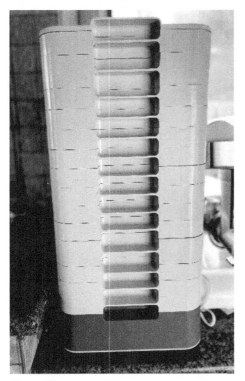

My current dehydrator, the L'Equip FilterPro (at last check, about $135 from Amazon), came with six stackable trays, six mesh screens, four yogurt containers, and two fruit leather trays. I now have fourteen trays (out of the fifteen maximum it supports), which come in handy at the height of apple season. I was also able to get additional fruit leather trays and yogurt containers from the manufacturer. I decided on this unit after attending a course from a very experienced dehydrator who owned both the L'Equip FilterPro and the Excalibur. She advised the class she preferred the lower cost, stackable L'Equip over the Excalibur. I have not regretted following her advice.

Bottom line, you can work with any dehydrator with separate time and temperature controls. Some may take longer to dry. Some may require you to dry smaller batches. However, all dehydrators the time and temperature will accomplish the goal. Buy the dryer that best fits your budget and your space.

Figure 33
L'Equip FilterPro dehydrator with 14 trays

Storing Dehydrated Foods

Storing your freshly dehydrated foods promptly is important to safe long-term storage. When your sun, oven, or commercial dehydrator stops producing heat, moisture starts to re-enter your food. Any level of moisture, however small, invites microbes to grow. Avoid the risk by being ready to package your foods as soon as they are dry.

With my commercial dehydrator, I intentionally set the time control for more hours than necessary to dry the food, as you cannot over-dry food. For example, I always check my dehydrator before bedtime and, if not ready to package, I add more than enough time to continue until I will be available to package the dried food items in the morning. If the unit has stopped before you arrive to check it, I recommend you turn it back on for one to two hours to ensure dryness before packaging. Check several pieces on each tray for dryness before packaging. If any pieces should signs of moisture, add time to continue the drying process.

Dehydrated foods must be stored in such a way that no moisture can enter the storage container. Store small amounts for short-term use in vacuum-sealed canning jars. The remainder should be stored in Mylar® bags for long-term use. Use of both packaging methods is detailed in Chapter 5.

Chapter 13
Dehydrating Tips and Resources

Getting started with dehydrating is easy. If you are uncertain about your interest in dehydrating long-term, consider experimenting with oven or sun dehydrating. With oven dehydrating, your only expense is the energy required to dry the batch. With sun dehydrating, if you use an old bed sheet as your drying surface, you will be able to experiment at no cost.

If you are serious about dehydrating, any of the dehydrators with separate time and temperature controls will work. While I recommend the L'Equip FilterPro, buy the best your budget will support that fits the space you have available.

My first experience with dehydrating was onions in my husband's round dehydrator. Fortunately, I had done some research before starting and learned not to dry onions (or their cousins) in the house. Drying onions produces strong odors that linger. Instead, we placed the dehydrator on the front porch, away from the front door, where we were fortunate enough to have an electric outlet. The only downside of drying a batch outside is dealing with humidity and, potentially, weather, either of which may necessitate additional drying time. Animals and insects could also be a problem, but I believe onion odor is offensive enough to ward off just about anything that might think about coming near!

Great Choices for Dehydrating

▶ Herbs

▶ Apples

▶ Fruit Leathers

▶ Yogurt

▶ Meat Jerky

Once I decided I was going to jump into dehydrating with both feet, I upgraded to the larger rectangular unit and put it to the test with apples. For my first apple run, I left the skins on and simply cut the apples (by hand) into thin slices. While the slices were tasty – and we ate every one – the skins became a little tough when dehydrated. For the next batch, I decided to peel the apples –

Figure 34
Stackable dehydrator with separate time and temperature controls

an arduous process when done by hand – but worth it as the final product was more satisfying. However, I knew there had to be a better way.

Enter the Victorio hand-cranked apple peeler. This little gem makes processing apples so much easier as it peels, cores and slices all at once, with only a few turns of the handle. With this labor-saving tool, I was able to process a full bushel of apples in only a few hours.

If your kids love fruit rollups, making healthy fruit leathers will appeal to you. Some dehydrators come with thin plastic trays for this purpose, but you can substitute parchment paper with the sides turned up to retain the fruit. In fact, it is actually easier to remove the finished product from parchment paper than from a tray. Puree the fruit(s) with a food processor or blender, spread on the tray or parchment paper, and place on a drying rack. The fruit leather, true to its name, will dry to a leathery consistency. The finished product can be cut into strips or rolled up.

Figure 35
Hand-cranked apple peeler, corer, and slicer

I do not dehydrate as much as I did before getting a freeze dryer. That being said, there are still some foods I always do in the dehydrator, such as herbs. Most herbs require only about six to eight hours at 110 degrees to dry. Freeze drying will use a lot more energy to accomplish the same goal. I dry most herbs on the stem, and then remove the individual leaves from the stem once dry. In fact, in some cases – such as with thyme and its tiny leaves – I may store it dried on the stem. If the leaves are large,

MY TOP 5 DEHYDRATING TIPS

▶ Store in small quantities to avoid moisture reabsorption issues

▶ Make sure to use the proper temperature for food type

▶ Test each tray for dryness – one moist piece will spoil entire package

▶ Rotate trays during dehydrating

▶ Allow extra time when humidity is high

however, such as with stevia or parsley, you may want to remove the leaves from the stems before drying.

Much to my surprise, my dehydrator came with four small plastic cups for making yogurt. I had absolutely no idea you could make yogurt in a dehydrator. To do so, you must have racks deep enough to accommodate the container in which you will make the yogurt. My dehydrator came with two trays deep enough for these yogurt containers and other large foods. If you do not have yogurt containers, you can also use quarter-pint canning jars, again assuming they will fit in your trays. I have included my yogurt recipe in Chapter 15.

Figure 36
Yogurt containers for dehydrator

I will be the first to tell you that I have never been the queen of jerky, and since I have acquired a freeze dryer, I must confess, I have not invested much time in improving my jerky-making skills. Use a lean cut of meat such as sirloin, top round, or bottom round. There are oodles of marinade recipes available. Marinade the meat, then place in the dehydrator at 155-160°F. For safety, when the batch is dry, place in the oven at 275°F to finish. You will find a couple simple jerky recipes in Chapter 15.

There are a few foods not suitable for dehydrating. These include avocado, blackberries, most dairy (including cheese and milk), and high-fat meats.

Figure 37
The Ultimate Dehydrator Cookbook

Dehydrating Resources

I have two resources I rely on for information on dehydrating. I really like the organization of *The Ultimate Dehydrator Cookbook* by Tammy Gangloff, Steven Gangloff, and September Ferguson. I find myself referring to this book virtually every time I dehydrate.

This book opens with three chapters on the basics of dehydrating, followed by sections on basic food types such as fruits, vegetables, jerky, and herbs. The back half of the book showcases recipes that utilize all the great dehydrated foods you can make.

My second go-to book is *The Dehydrator Bible* by Jennifer MacKenzie, Jay Nutt, and Don Mercer. This book has a wonderful quick reference for fruits and vegetables. There are also chapters on grains and dairy. This book includes a terrific chapter full of "just add water" recipes, and even man's best friend will find something to love with the chapter on dog treats.

However, it is not even necessary to buy a book, as there are a plethora of websites on dehydrating.

The National Center for Home Food Preservation, based at the University of Georgia, has an excellent free website, https://nchfp.uga.edu/how/dry.html. There are sections devoted to fruit leathers, vegetable leathers, fruits and vegetables, herbs, jerky, and more.

Figure 38
The Dehydrator Bible

If meat jerky is your focus, take a look at these websites:

https://www.jerkyholic.com

https://www.freshoffthegrid.com/simple-beef-jerky-recipe/

Great sites on dehydrating for camping include:

https://www.backpackingchef.com/

https://www.freshoffthegrid.com/backpacking-recipes/

Recommended sites for general dehydrating information are:

https://www.dehydrate2store.com/ - this is the website for my #1 recommended book above

https://www.freshoffthegrid.com/dehydrating-food/

Chapter 14
Dehydrating Step-By-Step

Each of the four dehydration methods – air, sun, oven, and commercial dehydrator – are detailed in depth in the sections below.

Air Dehydrating

Use this method for herbs, hot peppers, onions, garlic, shallots, and mushrooms only.

Herbs

Gather herbs in small bunches and tie the base of the stems together with kitchen twine, leaving enough extra twine to allow hanging.

Hot Peppers

You will need a large-eye sewing or yarn needle and kitchen twine. Tie a knot in the base of the string. String the peppers together by piercing the green cap at the top of the pepper with the needle. Leave space between each pepper to allow air flow between the peppers. Leave enough extra twine for hanging. Alternatively, if there are sufficient stems on the peppers you can use the method outlined above for herbs.

Onions, Garlic, and Shallots (Alliums)

Use the method outlined under Herbs above or braid the alliums into a string. Before braiding, allow the allium stems to dry for 7-10 days, either in the garden or on a counter. Do not allow the stems to become brittle before braiding.

Jill Winger, known as the Homestead Mentor, has a blog and YouTube channel, *The Prairie Homestead*. Before trying your first braid, I recommend watching Jill's instructional video, "How to Braid Onions to Make an Onion String" (https://www.youtube.com/watch?v=swoO6OyrqdI).[1] Seeing the braiding process is the best way to learn.

Mushrooms

Place mushrooms in a small paper bag. Gather the top of the bag together and bind with string, leaving a tail for hanging.

All Air Dehydrated Foods

Use the extra length of twine you left above to suspend the foods to be air dried in a location with good airflow where they can remain undisturbed until dry. Drying times will vary, depending on food type, temperature, and humidity.

Sun Dehydrating

Use this generally cost-free method for herbs, fruits, and vegetables only. Use in a grid down scenario, particularly when it is not possible to light an oven, or if energy consumption is a concern.

1. Determine the current humidity levels.

2. Review the weather forecast for the next three to four days. If humidity is expected to be greater than 60% during this period, review an additional one to two days of forecast. If precipitation or significant winds are expected during this period, consider delaying this batch or be prepared to suspend drying the batch until dry weather returns.

3. Prepare your drying surface (sheets, screens, etc.). Sheets (without frames) will need to be put in place first, and then loaded with foods. Frames can be loaded, and then placed in the sun.

4. Prepare the food(s) to be dried according to the guidelines for the food item. Try to maintain thin, uniform slicing to speed drying.

5. Load the drying surface with the slices of food, in a single layer. If using fabric as your drying surface, avoid overloading the surface. You need to have sufficient space to move your pieces around during drying.

6. OPTIONAL: If drying in the window of a vehicle, roll down the windows to allow airflow.

7. OPTIONAL: Cover the food with netting or cheesecloth to protect from insects. Anchor the edges with stones or weights.

8. Monitor sun position and adjust placement to maximize heating, if possible.

9. Monitor weather conditions. Bring food items indoors if adverse weather (precipitation or wind) threatens.

10. Turn slices every three to four hours, by hand or by using a spatula. If using a fabric surface, place in a new, dry spot, if possible, to allow the moisture in the fabric from the previous spot time to dry.

11. Bring food items and drying surfaces indoors before sundown to avoid the risk of condensation on the food items. Discard any pieces that show signs of mold.

12. Repeat the process daily until all slices are fully dried. Remove fully dried items daily.

13. Package dried slices promptly to avoid re-hydration.

Oven Dehydrating

Use this method for fruits, vegetables, herbs, and meat. This method can be used in a grid down scenario, when it is possible to light the oven and when energy consumption is not a significant concern.

1. Ensure sufficient time to complete drying operation, recognizing 12 or more hours may be required depending on temperature, humidity, air flow, and food(s) to be dried.

2. Wash and dry sufficient baking sheets to hold the foods you plan to dry. Multiple racks can be used for this process, increasing the number of baking sheets you can use at once. Insert extra racks, if available, to expand drying space.

3. OPTIONAL: Place a cooling rack on top of the baking sheet before loading food, to allow airflow all around the food item. If not using a cooling rack, line baking sheets with parchment paper or silicone mats for easy removal when dry.

4. Prepare the food(s) to be dried according to the guidelines for the food item. Try to maintain thin, uniform slicing to speed drying.

5. Preheat oven to 140-160°F, or as low as the oven is capable of being set.

6. Use the convection setting, if available, on your oven, as airflow is very important to achieve even and speedy drying.

7. RECOMMENDED: Validate the actual temperature with an oven thermometer.

8. Load the baking sheets with the slices of food, in a single layer. If you used a cooling rack with your trays, use extra care when moving, as the racks will slide very easily on the baking sheets.

9. Arrange the baking sheets in the oven.

10. Unless using a convection oven, leave the oven door open slightly. Use a wooden spoon, wood block, or silicone glove to prop the door, if it is not equipped to remain in a slightly open position.

11. OPTIONAL: If not using a convection oven, set up a fan adjacent to the partially open oven door to blow air into the oven. Moving air will dry more efficiently than still air.

12. Check the trays hourly, turning each piece over unless using a cooling rack.

13. Rotate trays periodically to promote even drying.

14. Repeat the process until all slices are fully dried. Drying may require 12 or more hours depending on temperature, humidity, airflow, and food item.

15. Remove fully dried items.

16. Package dried slices promptly to avoid re-hydration.

Commercial Dehydrator

Use this method for fruits, vegetables, herbs, and meat. The steps are the same regardless of type of dehydrator or number of trays used. Refer to your dehydrator's user manual for any special instructions unique to your device.

1. Wash and dry trays. Also wash and dry tray liners, if used. If not using tray liners, consider if parchment paper should be used to make it easier to remove the dried food from the tray.

2. Prepare the food(s) to be dried according to the guidelines for the food item. Try to maintain thin, uniform slicing to speed drying. Dry foods with strong odors alone!

3. Load trays with the slices of food in a single layer. Avoid loading too densely as air flow is critical to drying.

4. Stack or slide trays into dehydrator, depending on model. If using a stacking type dehydrator, remove any empty trays from the stack.

5. Set temperature as recommended for the type of food(s) being processed.

6. Set time as recommended for the type of food(s) being processed.

7. Check progress every four to six hours.

Figure 39
Apples on stackable dehydrator tray

8. If the food is very moist (e.g. apples or peaches) and/or there are a large number of trays being processed (greater than ten), consider rotating the trays at least once.

9. If using a stacked tray configuration, wipe excess condensation from the interior of the lid.

10. Check trays prior to going to bed or leaving the house. Add time, if required, to keep the dehydrator running until you can check it again.

11. Repeat until food is completely dry.

12. Package dried items promptly to avoid re-hydration.

Figure 40
Fully dehydrated apples,
ready to package

References

1. Jill Wagner, "How to Braid Onions to Make an Onion String", YouTube video, 5:40, November 6, 2018, https://www.youtube.com/watch?v=swoO6OyrqdI.

"It wasn't raining when Noah built the ark."
\- Howard Ruff

Chapter 15
Dehydrator Favorites

I hesitate to call these recipes, but this chapter includes preparation instructions for a few of my dehydrator favorites. Unless otherwise specified, all should be loaded on trays in a single layer. Drying times are approximate and will vary based on dehydrator, type of food, thickness of food, presence of skin, volume being dried, humidity, and ambient temperature. Add time as required to achieve full dryness, regardless of time specified in these instructions. It is common for me to run batches of apples, for example, for 16-18 hours, far in excess of the "standard" time to ensure dryness.

Herbs

Dry herbs at **110°F.**

Remove leaves from large or woody stems, leaving small stems intact.

Drying time varies, based on the herb.
- Basil   16-18 hours
- Mint   16-18 hours
- Rosemary   10-12 hours
- Oregano   10-12 hours
- Sage   12-14 hours
- Thyme   12-14 hours

Herbs are brittle and crumble easily when fully dried. Remove herbs from stems and package for storage.

Fruits

Apples

Dry apples at **130°F** for approximately **6-8 hours.**
I recommend Fuji apples, but experiment to find the varieties your family likes best.

Wash apples, especially if drying with skins on. Peel, if using in recipes.
Prepare lemon water solution (2 Tablespoons lemon juice in 2 cups cold water).
Peel and core apples one at a time, then cut into ¼" thick slices or rings.
Drop immediately into prepared lemon-water to prevent browning.
If drying more than 8-10 trays of apples at once, rotate trays every 4-6 hours.
In a stacked tray format, also wipe moisture from the interior lid of the dehydrator periodically.
Apples are dry when they snap in half easily and no trace of moisture is visible.

Bananas

Dry bananas at **130°F** for **8-10 hours**
I recommend firm, slightly (but not overly) green bananas.

Prepare lemon water solution (2 Tablespoons lemon juice in 2 cups cold water).
Peel bananas one at a time and cut into ¼" thick slices or 1/8" thick chips.
Drop immediately into prepared lemon-water to prevent browning.
Bananas will be brittle but slightly tacky when dry and must be peeled off the trays or liners.

Strawberries

Dry strawberries at **130°F** for **10-12 hours**

Wash and core strawberries, and slice ¼" thick.
Strawberries will be papery but remain slightly flexible when dry.

Kiwis

Dry kiwis at **130°F** for **10-12 hours.**
I recommend firm, but not hard kiwis.

Peel kiwis with a vegetable peeler, and slice ¼" thick.
Kiwi will be papery, but remain slightly flexible, when dry.

Vegetables

Carrots

Dry at **130°F** for **3-8 hours,** depending on format used (slices, thin slices, pieces, or grated).
Either whole or baby carrots can be used. Blanch before drying to maintain bright, orange color.

Wash and peel (if using whole carrots).
Thin Slices: Cut 1/8" thick. Blanch by dropping in boiling water for 1 minute, then remove and plunge into ice water to stop cooking. Dry 4-5 hours.

Slices: Cut 1/4" thick. Blanch by dropping in boiling water for 3 minutes, then remove and plunge into ice water to stop cooking. Dry 5-6 hours.

Pieces: Cut lengthwise, and then cut into pieces. Blanch by dropping in boiling water for 3 minutes, then remove and plunge into ice water to stop cooking. Dry 6-8 hours.

Grated: Grate directly onto trays covered with parchment paper or liners. Dry 3-4 hours.
Carrots are dry when crisp, but still slightly flexible.

Celery

Dry at **130°**F for **6-8 hours**.

Wash, and remove strings.

Slice 1/4" thick. Optionally, blanch by dropping into in boiling water for 1 minute, then remove and plunge into ice water to stop cooking.

Celery is dry when crisp, with no signs of moisture.

Mushrooms

Dry at **130°**F for **8-10 hours**.

Wash mushrooms. Remove stems, if desired. Slice 1/4" thick.
Mushrooms are dry when they snap in half easily, and there is no trace of moisture.

Garlic

Dry at **130°**F for **8-10 hours**. **HIGHLY RECOMMENDED: DRY OUTDOORS!**

Remove papery skins. Slice 1/8" thick, or mince.
Garlic is dry when brittle.

Onions

Dry at **130°**F for **8-10 hours**. **HIGHLY RECOMMENDED: DRY OUTDOORS!**

Remove outside skin.
Slice 1/4" thick or chop.
Onion is dry when brittle and no trace of moisture.

Yogurt

Dry at **115°F** for **6 hours**.
Makes 8 1/2 cup servings.

You will need yogurt containers made for your dehydrator, or quarter-pint canning jars. Make sure your dehydrator trays are deep enough to hold your containers! Sterilize containers or jars and lids.

4 cups non-fat milk
½ cup powdered milk
1 Tablespoon plain yogurt with active cultures (any fat content) to provide starter culture

Preheat dehydrator to 115 °F.
Dissolve powdered milk in liquid milk, whisking until smooth.
Heat to boiling, then remove from heat.

Active cultures are very temperature sensitive. Monitor temperature of milk mixture until it is below 120 °F, making sure it does not get below 100 °F.

As soon as the temperature drops below 120 °F, add the yogurt, and whisk until blended.
Ladle into containers or jars, and put on lids.
Place in preheated dehydrator. Dry for 6 hours.
Transfer to refrigerator, and chill for 8 hours.
For thicker, Greek style yogurt, drain off excess liquid.
Yogurt will keep for up to 1 month. Reserve 1 Tablespoon as starter for the next batch.
When ready to eat, add your favorite fruits.

PART FOUR
Freeze Drying

Chapter 16
What is Freeze Drying?

Freeze drying is a three-stage dehydration process utilizing extreme cold temperatures, vacuum pressure, and gentle heat to remove all moisture from foods and pharmaceuticals.

The earliest recorded use of freeze drying can be traced to the Peruvian Incas in the 1200s. Living at very high altitudes, the Incas discovered they could leave potatoes out at night to freeze, walk on them to squeeze out the ice crystals, and then leave them in the sun to dry. The resulting potatoes were very light, easily carried, and lasted a long time. An alternate process was to soak the potatoes in bitterly cold streams for several days rather than to freeze them overnight. Descendants of the Incas are still using these techniques today.[1]

The roots of modern freeze drying were sown in the early 20th century when several individuals simultaneously began to employ freeze drying in their scientific research. Leon Shackell, whose work was publicized in 1909, is most often regarded as the father of freeze drying. The advent of the first commercial freeze dryer in 1935, coupled with a newly developed technique for preserving blood serum through freezing and drying, enabled blood to be transported and stored, saving countless lives during World War II.[2]

While the use of freeze drying exploded over the subsequent 50 years, until 2013 freeze drying was strictly reserved for commercial, pharmaceutical, and military uses, due to the extremely high cost of the equipment, often hundreds of thousands of dollars.

In 2013, the first home freeze dryer was patented by HarvestRight and offered for sale at a price of $5000[3]. As of 2022, while the cost has come down significantly, HarvestRight remains the only freeze dryer available for the home market.

Why Freeze Dry?

Freeze dried foods will last at least 25 years when properly dried, packaged, and stored, contributing valuable resources for your food security. These foods retain most, if not all, of their original flavor and color and, more importantly, 97% of nutrients, although texture with some foods will be different. Ask any backpacker – freeze dried foods are incredibly lightweight and rehydrate more fully than dehydrated foods. You can store a lot more freeze dried food in the same space as commercially or home canned foods.

Food produced in a home freeze dryer is generally less expensive than commercially available freeze dried products. Blogger FamilyCanning.com has done extensive analysis on the cost effectiveness of freeze drying. Their detailed analysis, based on freeze drying frozen corn, shows it is cheaper to home freeze dry than to purchase commercially freeze dried #10 cans of corn, even though commercially freeze dried corn is often on sale and is typically a lower cost food item than many other commercially freeze dried foods[4].

Freeze drying allows you to avoid waste and spoilage in your regular daily life. Have some carrots nearing end of life that you will not be able to use in time? Freeze dry them. Tired of eating that leftover casserole that you made way too much of? Freeze dry it. You can virtually eliminate food waste for your household, if you choose to.

Freeze drying also gives you a couple of distinct advantages over dehydrating. You have the option of freeze drying some foods raw. Want to have fresh hamburgers or steaks on the grill during your next disaster? Freeze dry them!

So, if freeze drying is so great, why isn't everyone doing it? The number one reason is cost. As of this writing, the smallest unit available from HarvestRight lists for $2695. If you watch for one of their frequent sales, you might save $100 or more. Once in a blue moon, you might even find a used freeze dryer for sale, but do not expect to get much of a discount, given the demand. Wait times for a new unit have often reached six months.

If cost is not an issue, there are still other things to consider. Freeze drying is not a silent process. Even with the quieter oil-free pump, your new freeze dryer will be noisy. You will need to think carefully about where to place your unit. New owners who have put them in their kitchen or other primary living space have not been happy. I placed mine in my summer kitchen, a room created from a deck space off my kitchen. Since this was previously exterior space, this room has an R-33 insulated wall it shares with the living room, against which my couch sits. When the freeze dryer is running, it is necessary to increase the volume of the television to hear it clearly from the couch. Fortunately, we also maintained the exterior door that previously opened onto the porch. With this door closed, I can barely hear the unit running.

Thinking you will put your new freeze dryer in an extra closet or out in the garage? Think again. Another consideration with a freezer dryer is the amount of heat they produce. As I said, my unit sits in the open in the summer kitchen, but adjacent diagonally to our gas grill. While this space is insulated and has an HVAC duct, it will always be cooler than the rest of my house because there is an open deck beneath it. In fact, in the winter, I often place a small ceramic heater in the room to maintain the temperature. However, if my freeze dryer is running, it supplies all the heat I need for that room and then some! So much so that, if the freeze dryer is running and my husband is grilling for an extended period, my freezer dryer may overheat, interrupting my batch and requiring me to allow the unit to cool down before I can resume operation. If you live in Michigan, you may be able to operate your unit successfully in the garage. If you live in Arizona or Florida, probably not. I have read of numerous cases of overheating when units were set up in unconditioned spaces. Placement is everything. You will need to ensure adequate airflow, in a sound dampening space, maintained at a normal average room temperature.

You will need enough space to elevate both the freeze dryer and vacuum unit on a sturdy platform that will not be affected by vibration. The freeze dryer itself does not create vibration, but the attached vacuum pump will. Freeze dryers rely on gravity to drain the melted ice from the chamber after a batch is completed, so you will need to be able to place your catch basin – in my case, a bucket – below the bottom of the freeze dryer.

You will need to provide the proper electrical connections for your unit. For a small or medium freeze dryer, a 20 amp dedicated circuit is recommend, but not required. For a large unit, a 20-amp circuit is <u>required</u>. The need for a new dedicated outlet was one of the factors that led me to go with the medium.

Allow for an increase in your electric bill. Each load you process will run anywhere between 18 – 60 hours, depending on the age of your freeze dryer. My loads typically run 27 – 42 hours. I have not calculated the increase in my bill, but HarvestRight estimates approximately $1.25 - $2.80 per day for a small or medium and $2.00 - $3.00 per day for a large.[5]

With forethought, all of these considerations are manageable. While freeze drying is not for everyone, most of those who choose to pursue it become avid fans of the technology.

The Science of Freeze Drying

Back in high school science class, you learned about the three states of matter: solid, liquid, and gas. For example, ice (a solid) melts at 32 °F and becomes water (a liquid), which in turn becomes water vapor (a gas) at 212 °F. However, it is possible to go directly from a solid to a gas without passing through the liquid stage – a process known as sublimation.

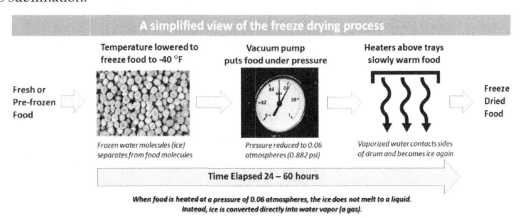

Figure 41
A Simplified View of the Freeze Drying Process

Freeze drying, or lyophilization, utilizes sublimation to remove water from food by maintaining an atmospheric pressure low enough to keep the water from liquefying, allowing ice to convert directly to water vapor. A three-stage process comprised of freezing, vacuuming, and drying, enables this process.

- In a home freeze dryer, the temperature is first lowered to 40 °F below zero, solidifying all of the water molecules in the food.
- Next, a vacuum is applied to remove all air from the freeze dryer, and to establish a pressure of 0.06 atmosphere or less (0.882 psi).
- At this temperature and pressure, the conditions are established to allow sublimation to occur.
- Heat is applied directly to the shelves that hold the food, warming them sufficiently to convert the ice directly to water vapor.
- The vacuum causes the water vapor to be pulled against the walls of the freeze dryer where the vapor condenses to ice once again.
- Over a period of hours to days, all of the ice is drawn from the food, rendering the food freeze dried[6].

References

1. Laurel Thompson, "Inca's Food Preservation – A Gift to the World – Part3", Kuoda Personalized Travel, September 27, 2019, https://www.kuodatravel.com/incas-food-preservation-a-gift-to-the-world-part3.

2. "Obituary of R I N Greaves, MD FRCP", *British Medical Journal*, 1990; 301:663, September 29, 1990, https://doi.org/10.1136/bmj.301.6753.663.

3. "Six Frequently Asked Questions about the Harvest Right Freeze Dryer", HarvestRight blog, accessed January 8, 2022, https://harvestright.com/blog/2020/six-frequently-asked-questions-about-the-harvest-right-freeze-dryer/#:~:text=The%20initial%20freeze%20dryer%20we,tariffs%20and%20increased%20component%20costs.

4. "3 Freeze Dryer Sizes Compared – Freeze Drying Corn", Family Canning blog, February 24, 2018, https://www.familycanning.com/freeze-drying-posts/cost-deep-dive/3-freeze-dryer-sizes-compared-corn/.

5. "FAQs: What Type of Power Do the Freeze Dryers Use? How Much Will It Cost To Run?", HarvestRight blog, accessed January 8, 2022, https://harvestright.com/faqs/.

6. Tom Harris, "How Freeze-Drying Works", How Stuff Works., accessed January 9, 2022, https://science.howstuffworks.com/innovation/edible-innovations/freeze-drying2.htm.

Chapter 17
Freeze Drying Tools and Methods

Choosing a Freeze Dryer

The choice of a freeze dryer is pretty darn simple: small, medium, or large. That is because there is currently only one home freeze dryer manufacturer, HarvestRight, located in Salt Lake City, Utah (https://www.harvestright.com). The deciding factor on freeze dryer choice is really how much you want to be able to freeze dry at a time, which ultimately determines how much you can process in a year.

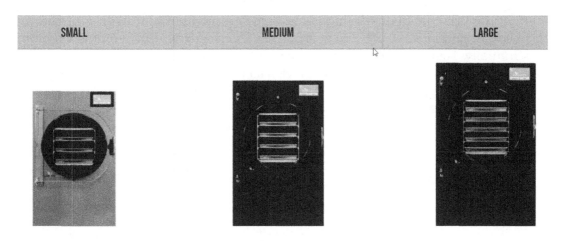

Figure 42
HarvestRight Freeze Dryer size comparison

As shown in the chart below, it is possible to process nearly three times as much food in a large as a small.

Characteristic	Small	Medium	Large
Number of shelves	3	4	5
Food input per batch (pounds)	4 - 7	7 - 10	12 - 16
Food output per batch (gallons)	1 - 1.5	1.5 - 2.5	2 - 3.5
Max input per year (pounds)	840	1450	2500
Max output per year (gallons)	195	312	546

As mentioned in Chapter 16, Blogger FamilyCanning.com has done extensive cost analysis on freeze drying. They did an excellent comparison between the three sizes of freeze dryers using frozen corn. Their analysis showed:

- The medium freeze dryer is 23% more cost efficient and 50% more time efficient than the small freeze dryer.
- The large freeze dryer is 10% more cost efficient and 41% more time efficient than the medium.
- A large freeze dryer can process more in a single batch than a small and a medium combined!

Their analysis clearly shows that, if your goal is to process as much food as possible, the large is the optimal choice[1].

To meet my personal freeze drying goals, I chose a medium unit. With four shelves, the medium gives me the best balance between batch size and the volume I can process annually. There have been times when I have looked around for *"what else I could freeze dry"* to fill out a batch. Had I purchased a large freeze dryer, which has one extra shelf and larger trays, I likely would have been in that situation much more frequently. If you need to freeze dry a tremendous volume of freeze dried food like the blogger of FamilyCanning.com who has eleven kids, a large is likely your best option. However, if you decide to go with a smaller unit for financial or other reasons, then focus on processing the high value and specialty items at home, and supplement your home freeze drying by purchasing lower cost commercially freeze dried items such as common fruits and vegetables[2].

The only other decision with the HarvestRight freeze dryer is which type of vacuum pump you want to use. The pump sits completely outside the freeze dryer cabinet – something that is not immediately obvious when you look at the pictures of freeze dryers on the HarvestRight website.

Two types of vacuum pumps are available: premier and oil-free. Older units, like my own, came with a standard pump, which is still available from HarvestRight, but is no longer the pump shipped with a new unit.

VACUUM PUMP PREMIER VACUUM PUMP LOW PROFILE OIL FREE PUMP OIL FREE PUMP

Figure 43
HarvestRight vacuum pump options

This table summarizes the differences between the three pumps, discussed in more detail below.

Characteristic	Standard	Premier	Oil-Free
Maintenance required	Yes	Yes	No
Oil required	Yes	Yes	No
Oil change frequency	4 – 5 batches	20 – 25 batches	N/A

Oil changes take less than five minutes. Some users will tell you the oil must be changed between every batch – and in fact HarvestRight used to recommend changing the oil after each batch. I have traditionally changed it after every other batch. HarvestRight now recommends changing every four to five batches with the standard pump. With a premier pump, that jumps up to every twenty to twenty-five batches. Or you can opt for one of the two more expensive oil-free pumps and forget about oil changes completely.

The premier pump, which is now the pump shipped with new units, requires the use of one of two specific oils: Robinair Premium High Vacuum Pump Oil or JB Industries Black Gold Vacuum Pump Oil. Use of any other oil will void the warranty. While either of these oils can also be used in the standard pump, many standard pump owners are using the much less expensive

Figure 44
"Homegrown" oil filter

Dairyland Vacuum Pump Oil, available by the gallon from Tractor Supply Company and many other retailers. This oil contains rust and oxidation inhibitors that help keep the pump in excellent operating condition. I have seen photos of the interior of pumps that used other oils compared to the interior of those using Dairyland oil and, while I cannot attest to the oil change frequency for any of these units, the difference was enough to convince me to use Dairyland. Thus far, I have not regretted my decision.

Understand that, while you must change the oil every few batches, you do not need to throw out this oil. Instead, you will filter the oil and reuse it in a future batch. I have run 30-35 batches on the same oil before I had to throw it out and start fresh. The original oil filter provided by HarvestRight was positively awful and this led HarvestRight owners to come up with their own innovations. One of these was so well-liked that an enhanced version of this customer-developed solution is now sold by HarvestRight!

To filter, you will need a container into which to drain your oil – I use an old bulk yogurt container. Additionally, you will need a filtering device and a funnel. The design I use is the aforementioned "homegrown" solution. I acquired a Brita water-filtering pitcher and gave away the original filter that came with the unit. I then fashioned a new filter from a roll of cheap single-ply toilet paper and used it in place of the original filter. When I replace my oil after 30-35 batches, I also make a fresh toilet paper filter. This filter works equally as well as the one now available from HarvestRight. I will cover the details of changing the oil in Chapter 19, Freeze Drying Step-by-step.

You will need a sturdy elevated surface large enough to hold both the freeze dryer and the pump. Keep in mind a medium freeze dryer weighs 120 pounds and has an 18" wide by 21.25" deep footprint, not including the vacuum pump that will need to sit right next to your unit. You will need a very sturdy, raised platform on which to place both the freeze dryer and the pump, as you will need to be able to use gravity to drain both oil and water from your unit. I purchased a stainless steel, food prep, commercial grade table. Without the casters, this table is rated to 300 pounds. With the casters (which I use), the rating drops to 150 pounds which is still enough to support the freeze dryer, pump, and accessories. A sturdy wood table or cabinet is also a good choice. It is critical the platform you choose can handle both the weight and prolonged

Figure 45
Sturdy cart supports freeze dryer and vacuum pump

vibration of the equipment. I have read several sad stories about support platforms that collapsed, causing the load to be lost, and badly damaging the freeze dryer. Check the stability of your platform regularly, retightening screws, if necessary!

Last, but not least, you will need a bucket which you will place lower than the freeze dryer, typically underneath, into which the drain hose will run to empty the melting ice from the unit at defrost time.

Accessories

None of the accessories listed below are required, but I have found all of these to be useful.

Door Pad

When I got my freeze dryer, each unit shipped with a door pad: a circular, insulated pad that just fit the front of the freeze dryer drum to help maintain ultra-cold temperatures in the machine. Subsequently, HarvestRight decided the pad was no longer needed and stopped shipping them with the unit.

Figure 46
Insulated door pad helps keep cold in

Many people—including myself—still believe they add value. HarvestRight no longer has them available for sale, but you can find individuals on Facebook or Etsy who make beautiful custom door pads.

Liners

Your freeze dryer will come with three, four, or five stainless steel trays (depending on size), upon which you will place your food for freeze drying. The tray dimensions increase with the size of the freeze dryer.

While you can place your food directly on the stainless steel trays, many – myself included – find it helpful to line the trays to make removal and clean up easier. I choose to use the reusable silicone liners available from HarvestRight, but many simply line their trays with parchment paper. Personally, I do not want to take the time to cut the parchment paper to fit or deal with the curling caused by the parchment paper rolls, but it is entirely a personal choice. The silicone liners are easy to use and wash off easily as does the tray. These have been one of my favorite accessories.

Figure 47
Trays provided with freeze dryer,
and optional silicone liners

Stackers

You will quickly discover freeze dryer trays take up a lot of freezer space (more about that in the next section). Two accessories allow you to stack the trays, greatly reducing the necessary freezer footprint. The first option, which is the choice I use, is a set of four plastic inserts that rest on each corner of a tray and allow another tray to sit securely on top. They come in sets, sized to your freeze dryer with enough pieces to allow you to stack all of your trays. I use this simple accessory nearly every time I pre-freeze my foods.

Recently, a set of lids was introduced, allowing you to cover the entire tray and then stack another tray on top. Had lids been available when I bought my stackers, I might have gone with lids, but again, it is personal preference. The lids can be put on faster

Figure 48
Freeze dryer trays with corner stackers

than the corner pieces but impose greater limits on the dimensions of items placed on the tray.

Small Trays

While some owners choose to buy a second set of full-sized freeze dryer trays (at no small cost, I might add!), I believe small trays are a more flexible, and definitely lower cost, alternative. Small stainless steel trays are very useful for preparing your foods for the freeze dryer, enabling you to pre-freeze food in smaller amounts, and then combine the frozen blocks onto freeze dryer trays. The optimal tray sizes will depend on which size freeze dryer you have. With a medium, I have found two sizes of trays to be helpful. With the smaller of the two trays, I can fit three blocks of frozen food to a tray. With the larger trays, I can just fit two to a tray. Depending on the foods, I sometimes instead use one large and one small together. Measure your trays and then search for the trays you find most useful for the types of food you plan to freeze dry.

Figure 49
Two sizes of small stainless steel trays

You may find these trays advertised under a variety of names. My larger trays are humorously considered "baking sheets" and came in a set of five 5" x 9" trays. The smaller ones are called "kids plates" and came as a set of two, that are 7.3" x 5.3" each. I have also seen similar trays advertised as "surgical trays".

Racks

Small baking/cooling racks are useful for increasing your yield per run with certain foods. For example, I use these racks when I process bananas, in order to dry two layers of non-frozen bananas without having them stick to one another. Two small racks (8.7" x 6.25") fit perfectly in a medium tray end-to-end, doubling my drying capacity. The ones I purchased from Amazon came as a set of three.

Figure 50
Two small racks on a medium freeze dryer tray (silicone liner beneath)

Silicone Molds

Figure 51
Variety of silicone molds used to pre-freeze in blocks

Silicone molds, in a variety of shapes and sizes, are extremely useful for shaping foods like applesauce, oatmeal, and yogurt into bite-sized snacks. Larger molds are useful for creating portions of casseroles or leftovers. Decorative molds, such as Halloween or Christmas themed molds, can be used to create fun treats such as freeze-dried eggnog bites. I recommend placing the molds on a cookie sheet or cutting board for stability <u>before</u> filling. Place in the freezer and freeze at least overnight. Once frozen, pop the segments from the molds. I recommend using gloves to protect your fingers. Place the frozen chunks onto a tray, leaving space around each for best results. You may want to save your pre-molded pieces in a Ziploc® bag in the freezer until you have enough for a full load.

Moisture Detectors

Moisture is the bane of a freeze dryer's existence. To help ensure optimum dryness, some owners use a moisture detector to help verify all moisture has been removed from the food on a tray at the end of the processing time. Some moisture detectors must be touched to the food in order to test for wetness. The type I use works by detecting temperature differences throughout the tray and does not require the device to contact the food. If one area of the tray is much colder than other portions, ice crystals likely remain in the food, and additional drying time will be required. If in doubt, add time!

Figure 52
One type of moisture detector

Gloves

A more recent addition to my tools is a set of inexpensive, thin, rubberized gardening gloves. I decided to add these after freezing my fingers, time after time, when handling my pre-frozen trays and molds. You will find it much more comfortable to eject segments from your molds and move trays from freezer to freeze dryer while wearing rubberized gloves.

Log Book/Sheet

I recommend keeping a log of each of your freeze dryer runs. This helps you keep track of the number of batches processed between oil changes, as well as the runtime for different foods. Record the date and time you start and finish each batch, along with the type(s) of food in the batch. This will allow you to predict drying times for future runs. While recipes provide a guide, drying times for the same food will vary based on your geography, weather conditions, and location of your dryer, in addition to variation introduced by the preparation of the batch. Record the date on which you change your oil. You can also keep track of when you replace your oil filter and when you throw out your old oil and start with fresh.

Additional Accessories

FrozenRight (www.frozenright.com) has many more accessories available, including racks to allow more efficient tray stacking, gadgets to make bag filling easier, and much more.

Freeze Drying Process

Food preparation varies widely based on food type. As with dehydrating, fruits that brown easily (bananas, peaches, apples, etc.) should be treated with citric acid, lemon juice, or FruitFresh. Blueberries need to have their skin pierced to provide a way for the moisture to escape. Grapes needs to be cut in half. Some vegetables such as potatoes, carrots, and green beans should be blanched for optimum results.

Any food can be pre-frozen, and some should always be frozen prior to freeze drying. For example, any foods you want to shape into molds, such as applesauce, yogurt, or oatmeal, will have to be frozen in order to maintain their shape as you do not freeze dry in the mold.

Pre-freezing will keep pieces of most foods from clumping. For instance, banana slices will stick to one another if they are freshly sliced and loaded in an overlapping fashion onto the tray. If, however, the slices are pre-frozen in a single layer, then they can be overlapped and loaded more densely onto the freeze dryer tray without fear of creating a lump of bananas. For this reason, I pre-freeze most of my fruits and vegetables.

Pre-freezing also allows you to build up enough food to run a batch. For efficiency, you really do not want to run a batch with empty or half-empty trays unless you have no other option at the time. I save leftovers on small trays and freeze them. Once frozen, I can transfer

Figure 53
Pre-frozen raw, beaten eggs

to a Ziplock® bag or freezer-safe container to hold in the freezer until I have enough for an entire batch, or until I need something small to fill out a tray to create a full batch.

Some foods simply process better when frozen. The most notable example is eggs. Many owners – myself excepted – have reported very messy batch failures when processing unfrozen raw eggs. Cleaning eggs out of the inside of your freeze dryer and all of the shelves is not fun. Pre-freezing the eggs has been shown to eliminate this type of failure.

Trays should be loaded with no more than 2.5 pounds of food per tray. The more densely the food is loaded on the tray, the longer it will take the batch to dry. As a rule, I load my foods in a single layer, with some exceptions for pre-frozen fruits and vegetables.

Multiple food types can be dried in the same batch, but care should be taken when drying foods with strong odors or flavors, such as onions or garlic. These should always be dried alone. If the scent lingers after the batch is completed, the unit should be wiped down with white vinegar to neutralize the residual odor before running another batch. For odors that hang on even after a vinegar wipe down, run a "waste batch" of bread and discard when complete, or run a batch of a complementary food. For example, after processing onions or garlic, I might process a batch of green beans because I always flavor my green beans with onion and garlic anyway.

If the foods have been pre-frozen, the unit will need to be turned on and the temperature lowered to freezing before the trays are loaded. For non-frozen foods, the trays can be loaded when the machine starts. Once started, the machine will run through the freeze, vacuum, and dry cycles with no operator intervention required. As with dehydrating, timely processing of a completed batch is important to maintaining the dryness of the freeze dried food items. Drying times can be extended, when required, to avoid batch completion during the middle of the night, when you will be away or when you feel extra time will be beneficial to ensure dryness. However, even if you fail to extend the drying time, the freeze dryer will automatically continue running to keep the unit frozen until you release the vacuum and advise the machine you are done.

When a batch is completed, never assume the batch is completely dry, no matter how many hours it has run. Always check the food by breaking a few pieces open – especially thick ones – to ensure the centers are dry. A moisture detector can be useful at this stage. If the batch is not fully dry, you will have the option of adding additional drying time. Repeat the process, as needed, until the batch is 100% dry. While the freeze dryer is designed to be able to detect automatically how long each stage of the process should run, there will still be times the batch needs more time. With experience – and the aid of your logbook – you will become proficient at estimating the run time for different types of food.

Once the batch is determined to be dry, the foods should be packaged in Mylar® bags with oxygen absorbers for long-term storage or in mason jars with oxygen absorbers for short-term storage. See Chapter 5 for details on sealing foods in Mylar® bags or in mason jars.

References

1. "3 Freeze Dryer Sizes Compared – Freeze Drying Corn", Family Canning blog, February 24, 2018, https://www.familycanning.com/freeze-drying-posts/cost-deep-dive/3-freeze-dryer-sizes-compared-corn/.

2. "3 Freeze Dryer Sizes Compared – Freeze Drying Corn".

Chapter 18
Freeze Drying Tips and Resources

Freeze drying is not for everyone. I had wanted a freeze dryer for more than two years before my husband surprised me with one as an amazing Christmas gift. The price is a showstopper for some. If that is the case for you, I recommend throwing yourself headlong into dehydrating instead. However, if your heart is still set on freeze drying and cost is a factor, consider whether you can find others in your area similarly inclined, and collectively invest in a freeze dryer that can be used by the entire group. You could rotate the unit physically from home to home on a monthly or quarterly basis, depending on how many owners were involved, or you could leave it in one place and rotate operators. Given the size and weight of a freeze dryer, moving it is honestly not very practical.

In some states, owners have been able to commercially market a portion of their output, helping to offset their cost of ownership. Research the laws in your state very carefully before embarking on this path, as some states prohibit cottage food sales entirely and others regulate it heavily.

Great Choices for Freeze Drying

▶ Eggs

▶ Cheese

▶ Ice cream

▶ Meat – including raw beef and pork

▶ Prepared meals

▶ Fruits

▶ Veggies

Alternatively, you could also pool your resources on the foods to be freeze dried and all take a share of each batch. I have a friend who has provided me with food from time to time and, in return, I provide her with a portion of the freeze dried output. As I always say, where there is a will, there is a way. You just might need to get creative to find it.

Once you have decided to move forward on a freeze dryer purchase, you might have to cool your heels for a while. Wait times for delivery often exceed three months, and have reached as much as six. If you just cannot stand the wait and do not mind driving, you may be able to call around to dealers in your regional area to see if any have units in stock. HarvestRight lists dealers on their website. The only caveat to this option is you may need to be flexible on your requirements for size, color, or type of pump, as you will be limited to what they have on hand. Online user groups are also great resources for used units. While most owners would not trade their freeze dryer for anything, a few decide it is just not for them and offer their unit for resale.

MY TOP 5 FREEZE DRYING TIPS

▶ Use pre-freezing to lower processing times and reduce failures

▶ Keep bags of frozen vegetables on hand for quick "fill-in" batches

▶ Use moisture meter to check dryness

▶ Package in Mylar with oxygen absorber for longest storage

▶ Re-tighten bolts on carts and other foundations supporting your unit

Use the time while you are waiting for delivery to handle electrical work (if required) and to get a good foundation in place. Keep in mind that, if you unit is being shipped directly from HarvestRight, it will be delivered to your curb – not to your door. It will be up to you to get it into the house and onto your foundation. Remember that these units between 63 and 161 pounds!

We live on top of a mountain where 4WD is essential. Curbside delivery for us meant meeting the semi-driver in a parking lot at the base of the mountain about 20 minutes away, transferring the unit to our SUV, and hauling it home ourselves. Once home, we had to wrestle the unit out of the vehicle, onto a dolly, and brute force it into the house. Even with two of us, lifting our medium unit from the floor onto the stainless steel cart I had selected as a foundation was a real chore. It slipped as we were trying to get it in place and very nearly landed on the tile floor where it (and likely the tile) would have been heavily damaged. Protect your investment. Make sure you have two or more <u>strong</u> sets of hands to get your unit to its final resting place.

Allow your unit to rest undisturbed for 24 hours after you have it set in place, then add oil to the pump (unless using an oil-free pump), and run the vacuum test outlined in your user guide. My unit failed this test miserably and it took several weeks of working with HarvestRight to solve the problem and ultimately pass this test.

Orange Side (heater) on top, facing down

Make sure the shelving unit that sits inside the drum of your freeze dryer is positioned correctly. The orange

Figure 54
Correct installation of shelving unit

heating units should be facing DOWN, not up, when the shelving unit is correctly placed in the machine. Position it to be as level as possible to avoid spillage from loaded trays.

Adjust the door hinge, if needed, to ensure you have a solid seal. With the rubber seal installed and the door fully latched, you should see a continuous narrow ring of contact between the door and the rubber. If there are breaks in this ring, adjust the hinge and recheck.

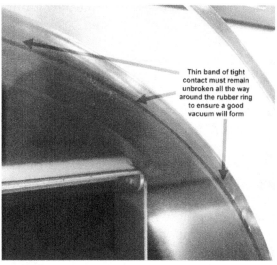

Thin band of tight contact must remain unbroken all the way around the rubber ring to ensure a good vacuum will form

Once you have established a vacuum, run a "waste batch" of bread through your machine, throwing it away once completed. This will help eliminate any odors lingering from the manufacturing process and will allow you to observe the freeze drying process, end to end, without worrying about the integrity of the load.

Figure 55
Proper door seal to achieve vacuum

If you opt for a vacuum pump that requires oil, do not scrimp on your oil changes, unless you like replacing pumps. Your vacuum pump is the heart of your system and requires maintenance to remain in good operating condition. Put your oil in the freezer to separate the water from the oil every time you perform and oil change. Even though water may not be evident when you remove the oil from the pump, freezing will prove to you that water is indeed present. Excess water in your pump will cause damage over time.

Resources

Unlike canning and dehydrating, there are essentially no books published yet on home freezing drying, except those of a scientific nature. This book is, in part, an effort to help fill that gap. There are, however, a few websites with information on home freeze drying.

❏ **Buying a Home Freeze Dryer: What to know before you go**
   https://digitalcommons.usu.edu/cgi/viewcontent.cgi?article=2999&context=extension_curall

❏ **Freeze Drying for Beginners**
   https://freezedryingmama.com/the-ultimate-freeze-drying-guide/

❑ **HarvestRight blog**
https://harvestright.com/blog/

Facebook groups dedicated to freeze drying are terrific resources for new and established freeze dryers alike. While new groups and pages spring up all the time, two of the most enduring groups are:

❑ **Retired at 40's Freeze Drying Group**
https://www.facebook.com/groups/retiredat40livelifesimple/

❑ **Betty's HarvestRight Freeze Dryers Group**
https://www.facebook.com/groups/BettysHarvestRightFreezeDryersGroup/

Similar groups may also be available on Instagram, Pinterest, and other social media sites. Search your favorite social media hangout for available groups.

The value of these resources is the ability to ask questions and get near real-time answers. More importantly, you can (and should!) search the questions previously asked and very likely come up with excellent information without needing to ask. For instance, when I processed my first batch of carrots, I searched for "carrots" on Betty's group and learned that I could preserve the orange color better by blanching my carrots first. These groups contain a wealth of information for both prospective buyers, as well as owners. Since these are moderated groups, the discussions remain, for the most part, on topic and pleasant.

Chapter 19
Freeze Drying Step-by-step

In this chapter, we will cover running a pre-frozen batch, a non-frozen batch, and changing the oil on an oil-based vacuum pump. Please note that sequence and instructions on the screen may vary based on the software version in use on the machine. Instructions below are based on software version 4.1.26. The latest available software version is 5.2.15. Significant differences between my version and version 5.2.15 are noted in italics. While I could upgrade to a later version of the software, I have been very happy with version 4.1.26, as it provides me an estimate of time remaining when I am in the drying cycle. The later versions (after 5.0) provide a progress bar rather than an actual time. I find I am able to plan more effectively when I know the number of hours left. As a result, I have elected not to upgrade my software. HarvestRight will provide alternate software versions, upon request. Be aware, however, the age of your machine may preclude running certain versions.

The instructions below assume you have already completed machine setup and vacuum pressure test as per the HarvestRight Owner's Guide. A copy of the latest Owner's Guide is available online at https://harvestright.com/support.

Care should be taken not to overload the trays. Foods should never extend more than ¼" above the top edge of the tray. Load no more than 2.3 pounds per tray in a small, 2.5 pounds per tray in a medium, or 3.2 pounds per tray in a large freeze dryer.

Instructions are provided for pre-frozen and non-frozen runs. Do not mix pre-frozen and non-frozen foods in the same batch.

- If you will be pre-freezing the foods for your run, complete the steps under Pre-frozen batch below, and then skip forward and continue with the steps under All Runs.
- If you are not pre-freezing the foods for your run, complete the steps under Non-frozen batch below, and then continue with the steps under All Runs.

Pre-frozen batch

1. Prepare the food(s) according to the best practices for each food item. Refer to Chapter 20 or search online freeze drying groups for best practices and recipes.

2. If pre-freezing directly on your freeze dryer trays:
   a. OPTIONAL: Line with silicone liners or parchment paper.
   b. Lay or spread the food on freeze dryer trays, keeping food level with the top of the tray.
   c. Place trays in freezer at least overnight, but 48 hours or more is recommended.

3. If pre-freezing on other trays or containers:
   a. Lay or spread food on cookie sheets or small trays in a single layer.
   b. Place trays in freezer at least overnight, but 48 or more hours is recommended.
   c. OPTIONAL: If you are working on accumulating enough pre-frozen food items for a run, transfer the food, once frozen, to a plastic bag or container until ready to run the batch. To remove frozen foods such as eggs or milk from smaller trays, run hot water over the back to release the frozen block from the tray.

Figure 56
Loading pre-frozen okra and leftover casserole slices

4. Turn on the freeze dryer using the rocker switch located on the back of the unit.

5. Once the unit has initialized, press Start, and then Pre-Frozen. Unit will cool for 30 minutes (to approximately 32°F) and then beep to alert you to add the pre-frozen trays.

   With later software versions, you no longer need to specify Pre-frozen. The unit will cool for 15 minutes then prompt you to add the trays. If 32°F is reached in less than 15 minutes, continue to the next step.

6. If food was not frozen directly on freeze dryer trays:
   a. OPTIONAL: Line with silicone liners or parchment paper.
   b. Load freeze dryer trays with pre-frozen food, keeping food level with the top of the tray. Foods do not need to remain in a single layer when they are frozen, but be careful not to overload.
   c. If freeze dryer is not yet ready to load by the time you have your trays prepared, place them back in the freezer to avoid thawing while waiting to load.

7. When unit signals it is ready, load trays.

Non-Frozen batch

1. Prepare the food(s) according to the best practices for each food. Refer to Chapter 20, or search online freeze drying groups for best practices and recipes.

2. For solid foods:
   a. OPTIONAL: Place silicone liners or parchment paper on freeze dryer trays.

Figure 57
From left, unfrozen beef bits, chicken, cheese, and potato corn chowder

b. Lay or spread the food on freeze dryer trays in a single layer.

c. OPTIONAL: For selected foods (such as thinly sliced fruits and vegetables), add a second layer by adding a rack(s) or parchment paper and another single layer of food. DO NOT OVERLOAD. Place trays in machine.

3. For liquid foods such as eggs or milk (*NOTE: pre-freezing highly recommended*):

a. Load trays into freeze dryer, leaving 2-3" of the tray exposed.

b. Support the tray with one hand and pour the liquid onto the tray.

c. Carefully push the tray the rest of the way into the shelf.

d. Repeat for remaining trays.

4. Turn on the freeze dryer using the rocker switch located on the back of the unit.

5. Once the unit has initialized, press Start, then Not Pre-Frozen, and then Liquid or Non-liquid as appropriate. *With later software versions, you no longer need to specify Pre-frozen and Liquid / Non-liquid.*

All runs

1. Insert insulator pad, if using, then close and latch door fully to the second latch position. Visually inspect to ensure pad placement did not affect door seal, and that door shows good contact with the black rubber ring all the way around. Refer to Figure 55 in Chapter 18 for an example.

2. Close valve on drain tube.

3. Press Continue.

4. Machine will freeze, vacuum, and then dry the batch, without additional operator intervention.

5. Check the display periodically for any error messages, and monitor the time remaining on the batch. *Newer software versions will not display a specific time, but rather a status bar indicating how complete the batch currently is.*

6. If batch is projected to finish while you will be away or asleep, add time to allow it to finish at a more appropriate time.

7. When time has expired, make sure the drain hose is out of the bucket or the bucket is completely empty before opening the drain valve to release the vacuum pressure. Failure to ensure the drain hose is out of the water before opening the drain valve will result in water being sucked back into the freeze dryer, ruining the batch. Note: There is an inexpensive "Y" valve available from FrozenRight (www.frozenright.com) which can prevent this problem from occurring.

8. Open the door and remove one tray to check dryness. Break open several of the thickest pieces to feel and inspect the center. If using a moisture detector, check the broken sides of the piece to verify the center is dry. If using visual inspection only, look and touch the center of both pieces to gauge dryness. Check multiple pieces.

9. If any portion of the tray is not fully dry, replace the tray and select More Dry Time. If the pump had just stopped when you arrived to check the batch, the pump may need to go through an approximately one hour cooling cycle before it starts to dry again, and will begin running with a default of two hours additional dry time. If the batch ended at least one hour before you began inspecting the batch, the cooling cycle, if needed, will already be complete. Once the cooling cycle has finished (if applicable), the dry time can be adjusted to add more than two hours of additional drying time. Keep this potential delay in being able to extend the dry time in mind if checking a batch just before bedtime or before leaving the house. Failure to allow sufficient time for the cooling cycle to occur may make it impossible to set the dry time for longer than the default two hours.

10. If fully dry, package the contents of the tray in Mylar® bags or canning jars with oxygen absorbers. Seal Mylar® bags with an impulse sealer. Label bags or jars.

11. Once the contents of all trays are packaged, close the door and select Defrost, making sure the drain hose in placed into a bucket or other container to catch the drainage from the melting ice.

12. Once the defrost cycle is complete, discard the water in the bucket.

13. Wipe down the interior of the machine and each shelf with water or white vinegar.

14. Change oil, if required. (See step-by-step process below.)

Changing the Oil

1. Gather the required tools:
   a. paper towel
   b. used oil container with lid suitable for freezing – I use an empty large yogurt container
   c. filter device
   d. funnel
   e. new oil (if needed), or previously filtered oil

2. If oil has been previously drained, and the used oil container already contains oil:
   a. Remove used oil container from freezer

Figure 58
Oil Filter available from HarvestRight

116

b. Pour thickened oil from used oil container into top of filtering unit

c. Use a table knife to loosen accumulated ice from bottom of used oil container, and discard.

3. Place used oil container under drain spigot.

4. Remove stopper and O-ring from oil fill location, and set aside.

5. Rotate valve to allow oil to flow from machine into used oil container.

6. Once flow of oil slows, tip pump to 45 degrees to fully drain oil. Return gradually to level, allowing oil to continue draining into container.

7. Once flow of oil stops, close valve and wipe any residual drips with a paper towel.

8. Place lid on used oil container, and place into freezer until next oil change.

9. Place funnel into oil fill location.

10. If oil has been previously filtered and is clean enough for reuse, pour oil from filter pitcher into pump using the funnel. As mentioned earlier, I can typically recycle the same oil through 30-35 batches when I changed the oil every other batch. If no recycled oil is available, or it is time to replace the oil completely, pour new oil into pump.

11. Fill until oil reaches fill line on oil view window.

12. Remove funnel and replace oil fill cap, insuring O-ring is in place.

13. Set filter pitcher aside to allow oil to filter from top section into the bottom portion of the oil filter pitcher. Filtering will take longer when the filter medium is new.

NOTE: Discard oil that appears dirty after filtering. Replace filter medium periodically. I replace my filter when I discard the oil to start with fresh oil again.

"Learn to sustain yourselves; lay up flour and grain and save it against a day of scarcity." - Brigham Young

Chapter 20
Freeze Dryer Favorites

This chapter contains guidance on processing some of my favorites in the freeze dryer. It is not an exhaustive guide, but includes general guidelines for each category so you can utilize them for similar foods not covered in this brief guide.

Pre-freezing is recommended, but optional, although I have noted those instances where it is <u>highly</u> recommended.

Processing times will vary based on your specific machine, the ambient temperature and humidity, the food item, how it is prepared, and whether it is pre-frozen or not. Remember that the machine will decide how long it believes the batch needs to run by sensing dryness. Timeframes, where provided, simply indicate my experience with that type of food. Individual results will vary.

Fruits

In general, fruits should be cleaned, then sliced or chunked. Fruits that brown when exposed to air (e.g. bananas, apples, peaches, pears, etc.) should be treated with citric acid, lemon juice, or FruitFresh immediately after slicing. Unless pre-frozen, place fruits in a single layer to minimize sticking.

<u>Apples</u>

My not-yet-two-year-old granddaughter tells her parents to "Call Granny. Apples!" when she runs out of my Fuji slices, freeze dried every fall from the bounty of our local orchard.

Whether you leave the peel on or not is strictly personal preference. My first batch of apples were peel on and sliced into small wedges. While very good, the peel dries slightly tougher than the body of the fruit. All subsequent batches have been peeled and sliced to 1/4". Using a hand-cranked Victorio apple peeler/corer/slicer (see Chapter 13, Figure 35) makes this a fast and easy process.

Wash apples, especially if drying with skins on. Peel, if using in recipes. Prepare lemon water solution (2 Tablespoons lemon juice in 2 cups cold water). Peel and core apples one at a time, then cut into ¼" thick slices or rings. Drop immediately into prepared lemon-water to prevent browning

I have processed apples both pre-frozen and not pre-frozen, and the results have been the same. One advantage to pre-freezing is a slightly increased yield since, once frozen, the apple slices can overlap allowing more per tray.

Average runtime: 27 – 32 hours

Bananas

Freeze dried banana chips make a great snack or add to your favorite cereal for a morning treat. I recommend firm, slightly (but not overly) green bananas.

Prepare lemon water solution (2 Tablespoons lemon juice in 2 cups cold water).

Peel bananas one at a time and cut into ¼" thick slices or 1/8" thick chips.

Drop immediately into prepared lemon-water to prevent browning.

I have processed bananas both pre-frozen and not pre-frozen, and the results have been the same. One advantage to pre-freezing is a slightly increased yield since, once frozen, the banana slices can overlap allowing more per tray. Or use small cooling racks (see Accessories in Chapter 17) to process two layers of fresh banana slices.

Average runtime: 27 – 32 hours

Blueberries

The thick skin on fresh blueberries makes it very difficult for moisture to escape. The only way to process fresh blueberries successfully is to either slice the berries in half, or pierce the skin on each blueberry with a pin, knife, or other sharp instrument, so moisture has a way to escape. If processing large batches, this is a tedious process. Expedite by using an implement capable of piercing multiple blueberries at once. A very efficient (but expensive) device, the Berry Roller, is available from FrozenRight (www.frozenright.com). Inexpensive alternatives include meat tenderizers with long tines, or tools used to hold vegetables for slicing. Alternatively, blanch fresh blueberries for 1 minute to pop skins. If you are processing frozen blueberries, placing them in a Ziplog® bag and striking them lightly with a meat tenderizer will pop the skins.

Do not overload the trays, as the high moisture content will lead to excessively long run-times.

If you are processing blueberries to make blueberry power, pre-process the berries in a blender or food processor prior to freeze drying to eliminate the need to pierce individual blueberries.

Average runtime: 50-60 hours

Grapes

Use only seedless grapes. Wash. Cut in half or blanch to pop the skins. Grapes may be pre-frozen in a single layer, if desired. Pre-frozen grapes may be overlapped when loading trays to go into the freeze dryer. If loading fresh grapes, load in a single layer to avoid clumping.

Average runtime: 50-60 hours

Mandarin Oranges

Either canned or fresh mandarin oranges can be freeze dried. When using fresh, care must be taken to remove all of the white membrane, which will turn bitter when freeze dried, if not fully removed. A pectin enzyme, such as Pectinex, can be used to easily dissolve the membrane. Due to the high moisture content, all citrus will require extended runtimes.

The peels can also be freeze dried and powdered to create orange zest.

Average runtime: 55-60 hours

Pineapple

Canned or fresh pineapple may be used. When processing canned pineapple, I like varieties with no sugar added. Peel, core, slice, and chunk fresh pineapple into the desired size.

Average runtime: 44-48 hours

Peaches

Canned, frozen, or fresh peaches can be used. When processing canned peaches, I like varieties with no sugar added.

Fresh peaches should be blanched to remove the skin. Place 2 cups of cold water in a bowl and add 2 tablespoons lemon juice. In another large bowl, add cold water and ice cubes to make an ice bath. Cut an X on the bottom of each peach and place in boiling water for 1 minute to loosen skin. Remove from heat and place into prepared ice bath. Skin will slip off easily. Pit and slice peaches, then place immediately into prepared lemon water for 3-5 minutes to prevent browning.

Pre-freezing is optional, but doing so will allow you to process more per batch, as pieces may overlap without the risk of clumping.

Average runtime: 32-36 hours

Strawberries

With a large strawberry farm just down the mountain from us, I process as many strawberries as I can each spring. Freeze drying preserves the rich red color far better than dehydrating or canning.

Wash, core, and slice. Pre-freezing in a single layer will allow you to load more fruit per tray than if not frozen.

Figure 59
Strawberries, at completion of freeze dryer cycle

Average runtime: 24-27 hours

Watermelon

To me, freeze dried watermelon tastes like cotton candy and simply melts in your mouth! I package in mason jars because watermelon never stays around long enough to make it to our long-term storage!

Cut into bite sized chunks, removing any seeds. Pre-freeze, if desired, although I have usually processed non-frozen.

Average runtime 42-44 hours

Vegetables

In contrast to fruits, vegetable preparation varies widely. Vegetables should be blanched before freeze drying, regardless of whether they will be processed pre-frozen or fresh. Blanch most vegetables in water, then plunge into an ice bath to stop the enzymatic reaction. Broccoli, sweet potatoes, pumpkin, and winter squash should be steam blanched, rather than being blanched in water. For vegetables not included below, treat as you would for freezing, or search one of the freeze dryer groups listed in Chapter 18 under Resources to find best practices on processing the vegetable you are interested in freeze drying. Shop your local Sam's Club or Costco for great deals on canned vegetables in bulk (#10 cans).

Corn

Frozen corn is one of my favorite things to process because it is an inexpensive way to expand my food storage. A 2-pound bag of your store brand corn will just fill a medium freeze dryer tray. For $10, or less if I watch for sales, I can store 8 pounds of freeze dried corn in a little over a day.

Canned corn is another option, especially if you can tap into sales. Pre-freeze, if desired.

For fresh corn, blanch for 7-11 minutes (depending on ear size,) or cook fully on the cob then remove kernels. Pre-freeze, if desired.

Average runtime: 30-32 hours

Green Beans

Freeze dried green beans make a tasty snack alternative to chips. Consider tossing with sea salt prior to freeze drying.

Blanch fresh green beans for 3 minutes prior to pre-freezing to preserve color and avoid toughness. Green beans can also be fully pre-cooked prior to processing.

Frozen green beans are easy to process. A 2-pound bag of green beans will just fill a medium tray. Canned green beans, including French style and Italian green beans, are great options. A #10 can of green beans will fill two medium freeze dryer trays. Pre-freeze, if desired.

Average runtime: 36-40 hours

Mushrooms

Wash mushrooms thoroughly. Remove stems, if desired. Slice. Pre-freeze in a single layer, if desired. Pre-frozen mushrooms may be overlapped when loading trays for the freeze dryer. If processing fresh, arrange in a single layer to avoid clumping.

Average runtime: 32-36 hours

Onions, Garlic, and Shallots

Slice, dice, chop, or mince onions, garlic, or shallots. Pre-freezing can help minimize (but not eliminate) lingering odors in your freeze dryer after processing. Bags of frozen, chopped onions from your grocery store's freezer section can also be used to speed processing (and minimize crying). Frozen onions produce less odor in the freeze dryer than fresh.

After completing the batch, wipe down the interior of the unit, shelves, and trays with white vinegar to help eliminate odor. I recommend following an onion, garlic, or shallot run, with a run of a vegetable such as green beans or peas that you might normally season using onions, garlic, or shallots. In this way, if the vegetable picks up some odor or flavor from the allium, it will enhance, rather than detract, from the food. If the odor persists after wiping with vinegar and you do not plan to run a compatible vegetable, run a batch of bread, and discard.

Average runtime: 38-42 hours

Peas

Frozen peas is another of my favorite things to process. It is an inexpensive way to expand my food storage because peas can be combined with so many other foods to help make a meal. A 2-pound bag of your store brand peas will just fill a medium freeze dryer tray. For around $10, I can store 8 pounds of freeze dried peas.

Canned peas is another option, especially if you can tap into sales or bulk sizes. Pre-freeze, if desired. For fresh peas, blanch or cook, then pre-freeze, if desired.

Average runtime: 30-32 hours

Peppers

Slice, dice, or mince peppers, based on your intended usage. Pre-freeze, if desired.

Figure 60
Sliced peppers ready for freeze drying (above), and after freeze drying (right)

Average runtime: 36-40 hours

Potatoes

To avoid having potatoes turn black when frozen, always blanch 5-6 minutes or cook potatoes, prior to pre-freezing or processing. Potatoes can be sliced, cubed, diced, shredded, or mashed, depending on your intended use when rehydrated.

For mashed potato flakes (aka instant potatoes), boil, peel, and mash with a potato masher, prior to freeze drying. Create potato flakes by running finished potatoes through a food processor before packaging. Do not add butter prior to freeze drying. The added fats will dramatically shorten shelf life.

To make shredded potatoes for hash browns, you can either bake the potatoes fully, cool, peel, and shred, or peel and shred raw potatoes, and then blanch for 3 minutes.

Average runtime: 28-32 hours

Dairy

Being able to safely process dairy products is one of the many benefits of freeze drying. Milk, cheese, yogurt, and more can all be safely processed. The fat content in cream, however, is too high to allow for stable storage. If you are processing a ready-made item with a small amount of cream used as an ingredient, you may be all right, but processing of pure cream is not recommended.

Cheese

I LOVE cheese! I was delighted to discover that I could freeze dry cheese in many forms.

One of the simplest is shredded cheese. Just open a bag of your favorite shredded cheese (or shred your own), and spread in an even layer on your tray. Pre-freeze, if desired, although I usually do not.

Slices of hard cheese – or even cheese sticks (whole or sliced) – make wonderful snacks. I keep these in my desk drawer for a quick bite of protein.

Crumbled feta or blue cheese also works (and snacks) well. Even cream cheese can be freeze dried. Crumble by hand to a powder for storage.

Rehydrating tip: Drizzle water into ¼ cup of cream cheese powder and stir to achieve desired consistency.

Average runtime varies depending on type and volume, but in general should not exceed 32 hours

Ice Cream Sandwiches

For a fun treat, try ice cream sandwiches. No need to rehydrate these little gems. Just pop one in your mouth for an amazing treat you will not be able to stop eating!

Ice cream is one of those foods prone to messy "explosions". The key to avoiding a catastrophe is keeping your ice cream sandwiches hard-frozen, and only loading them into a sub-freezing machine. Some owners have reported specific brands as being more reliable than others. Personally, I believe the temperature of both the bars and the freeze dryer is the bigger factor in a successful run. That being said, I use PET Light Ice Cream Sandwiches. I unwrap each bar and cut into roughly 30 bite-size pieces. Once cut, I return the pieces to the freezer to fully re-solidify before processing. I have yet to have a mishap. (Knock on wood!) Others have processed their ice cream sandwiches whole, halved, or quartered. They can be wrapped or unwrapped, but if wrapped, open the wrapper, or cut 3-4 slits to allow airflow.

Average runtime: 46-50 hours

Eggnog

Finding leftover eggnog in the refrigerator after the holidays one year, I decided to experiment with holiday silicone molds and discovered a great way to make festive Christmas treats. Place the molds on a tray, then fill, and freeze. When solid, pop out and store in a plastic bag until you have sufficient quantity to process a batch. Place in a single layer, not touching, on the tray.

Average runtime: 36 – 40 hours

Milk

Any type of milk can be processed – cow, goat, almond, oat, coconut, and even breast milk. Any fat content is acceptable, although shelf life may be longer with lower fat varieties. Cream, as previously mentioned, does not work well due to the high fat content.

While I have been fortunate enough to have processed my 2% milk without pre-freezing, I have read many, many horror stories from those whose milk run "exploded" coating their entire freeze dryer in a foamy white mess. Therefore, it is highly recommended that you pre-freeze your milk before processing. I do not know of any instances where a pre-frozen batch has suffered this fate.

Use care when placing trays of liquid into your freezer. I recommend freezing in small trays that are more easily manipulated, rather than in the large freeze dryer trays themselves.

Average runtime: 36-40 hours

Yogurt

Regular yogurt yields a better product than Greek yogurt, which tends to become chalky or powdery. Fill silicone molds with yogurt or create drops by cutting the corner from a plastic bag and squeezing yogurt onto a tray. Pre-freeze. Drops will dry faster than molds.

Add-ins for yogurt include pureed fruits, Cool Whip, or cream cheese, all of which create a less chalky outcome. My husband, upon eating a single plain Greek yogurt drop, proclaimed his mouth felt like the Sahara desert. I, on the other hand, mixed just a little water with several of the yogurt drops and found they reconstituted to a very similar consistency as the original yogurt.

Average runtime: 30-36 hours, depending on shape and add-ins

Proteins

Chicken

Chicken is the #1 meat I process, due to its low fat content. Not only is it healthy, but its leanness also means it will be more shelf stable than higher fat meats. <u>Never</u> **freeze dry raw chicken.**

Cook chicken thoroughly, ideally by baking or boiling, to eliminate as much fat as possible. I cut boneless, skinless breasts into chunks about 1/2" thick, and boil for about 45 minutes, skimming off the foamy fat released during the boiling process. Once cooked thoroughly, I place the chunks onto cookie sheets or small trays in a single layer, and pre-freeze, at least overnight. I also cut some into small bits to use as very popular dog treats, some of which are ultimately powdered to make "fairy dust", the magic top dressing that makes even finicky dogs lick their bowls clean!

Average runtime: 42-46 hours, depending on thickness of chicken slices

Eggs

As discussed in Chapter 4, eggs are the most inexpensive and compact protein you can store. Personally, I do not think you can ever have too many eggs in storage. **Always pre-freeze eggs.** Yes, some people, myself included, have successfully processed them non-frozen, but after learning of the significant risk of "eggsplosion", I now pre-freeze in small trays. I learned to use the small trays the hard way, after cleaning egg, spilled from my full-sized freeze dryer trays, off the bottom of my deep freeze. Once frozen, I release the "eggcicles" from their trays and store them in plastic containers until I have enough for a full run.

I can fit the equivalent of 18 eggs per medium tray. I crack them all into a large measuring cup and whisk to blend as smoothly as possible, before pouring onto the small trays. You may find it easier to place the tray in the freezer first, and then fill, or, alternatively, to fill the trays partially, then top off the tray once placed in the freezer.

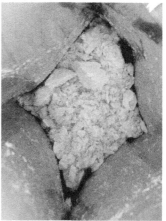

Figure 61
Whole eggs, after freeze drying - pre-frozen in small trays (above) and powdered for storage in Mylar® bag (right)

Some will put the finished batch of eggs through a blender or food processor, but I do not believe this is necessary. I simply crush into smaller chunks by hand, as I place them into the Mylar® bags. I recommend storing in smaller increments. I keep some of this egg powder in a half-pint jar to use in case I run out of fresh eggs. They are great scrambled, or used in cooking.

Rehydrating tip: Two tablespoons of egg powder and two tablespoons of water is the equivalent of one whole egg.

Average runtime: 36-40 hours

Ground Meats (any type)

The key to successfully freeze drying and storing ground meats is leanness. Choose high quality meats with low fat content. Ground beef, chicken, mutton, pork, turkey, veal, and venison are all candidates. For ground beef, opt for 90-10 (lean/fat) or even 93-7, instead of the less expensive 80-20 versions.

Cook meat thoroughly. Drain and rinse well in warm water to remove fat adhered to the cooked meat. Pre-freeze, if desired.

Average runtime: 40-44 hours

Luncheon Meats

For thin or medium thickness meats, roll into small tubes, which will store better without crumbling. Arrange in a single layer on a tray, without touching, and pre-freeze.

For more thickly sliced meats, process pieces in a single layer to avoid sticking.

For best results, rehydrate with the minimum water necessary, or wrap rolls in a damp paper towel in the refrigerator.

Average runtime: 40-44 hours

Steak

Remember that your steak should protrude no more than ¼" above the top of your freeze dryer tray. Choose your steaks carefully. Pre-freeze raw steak before processing.

Rehydrating tip: marinade overnight in beef broth to enhance flavor. Steaks can be pan-seared, grilled, or sous vide, just as fresh steaks are cooked.

Average runtime: 46-50 hours or more, depending on thickness

Miscellaneous

For the most part, you are limited only by your imagination. Virtually any food can be a candidate to freeze dry, with the exception of high-fat items such as fatty meats, cream, and chocolate. If in doubt with regard to how well a particular food will freeze dry, try processing a small amount, then reconstitute, and sample. If you are concerned about how long it will store, plan to sample the item in a pre-determined amount of time after freeze drying, to determine how well it stores.

Banana Bread

With just a little space left over on a tray, I decided to experiment by running small cubes of leftover banana bread. Yum! I had similar results with chocolate scones as well as a chocolate rum cake left over from Christmas dinner.

The finished product will be crunchy, like a brittle cookie with excellent flavor. I have also heard they are excellent dunked in coffee or tea, like a biscotti.

Cut bread into small cubes. Pre-freeze cubes, if desired.

Average runtime: 28-32 hours

Applesauce Bars

These are, without a doubt, my favorite freeze dried treat.

Pour your favorite applesauce into small silicone molds. I use no-sugar added applesauce, both store bought and my own home canned variety. The molds I use are mini-bars, approximately ¾" wide and 2" long. Stir in cinnamon, if desired, before filling molds.

Freeze solid, then pop bars from molds. Store in a Ziplock® bag or other freezer container until you have frozen enough for a batch. Place on trays in a single layer, without touching.

Figure 62
Preparing applesauce bars for the freeze dryer

Average runtime: 32-36 hours

Oatmeal bars

Use your imagination with these treats, starting with plain oatmeal or your favorite flavored oatmeal packet.

Make oatmeal according to the usual directions. Stir in pureed fruit or yogurt, if desired, and then fill silicone molds to create full-sized or miniature bars. Freeze, pop out of molds, and store until you have sufficient volume for a batch.

Finished bars can be eaten as-is for a snack, or place one or more bars in a bowl and rehydrate for a ready-to-eat oatmeal in the flavor of your choice.

Average runtime: 36-40 hours

Leftovers

Just about any leftovers you have are a candidate for the freeze dryer. Do consider the fat content of the food, as this will affect how long the food can be stored. Leftovers are a place where those small trays particularly shine.

Fill up a tray with a leftover serving or two of a casserole, one-pot meal, vegetable, or soup. Freeze. Once solid, pop out the block of frozen food and store in a plastic bag or container until you have sufficient volume for a load. Or, grab a block from the freezer to fill out a not-quite-full tray on your next batch.

Appetizer, main course, side, or dessert can all go into the freeze dryer, eliminating waste and adding to your long-term storage, one meal at a time. Just make sure you label the finished product well to avoid future surprises!

Average runtime will vary

PART FIVE
Getting Started

Chapter 21
Where Do I Begin?

Start (or re-start) your food security journey by completing the worksheets in Part One of this book, if you have not already done so. These will help you establish or affirm your food security goals. The vast majority of those who have wisely begun to build their long-term food security have unwisely done so, without considering their actual needs. If that is you, now is a great time to take a step back and build your plan before continuing on your journey. If you have not yet begun your journey, there is no time like the present to build your plan. It does not cost you a thing to create a plan, but it can save you time and money as you put that plan into action. Do not try to do this in your head. Commit your plan to paper and refer to it often.

Once documented, you can consider how to go about executing against your plan. Use the comparison shown below, along with your completed worksheets, to determine which of the methods are most appropriate for you at this stage of your journey.

	Canning	**Dehydrating**	**Freeze Drying**
Cost of entry	Low	Low - Medium	Very High
Cost per batch	Low	Low	Low
Time per Batch	30 minutes – 3 hours	10-18 hours	24-60 hours
Shelf Life	2-3 years	5-7 years	25+ years
Nutritional Value Lost	60-80%	5%	3%
Ideal for...	Fresh	Fresh, canned, or frozen	Fresh, canned, or frozen

Choose one of the four paths below based on your current level of experience with food preservation:

- I am brand new to all food storage methods
- I store commercially prepared foods
- I am using one or two of these methods
- I am using all of these methods

I am brand new to all food storage methods

Terrific! There is no time like the present to begin, even if your first step is simply buying one more can of green beans or another package of rice on your weekly grocery run and setting it aside to begin chipping away at your food security goals.

If you aren't ready to start using these do-it-yourself methods but want to more actively store, buy #10 cans of commercially freeze dried or dehydrated foods from reputable manufacturers like Emergency Essentials, Mountain House, Augason Farms or Thrive Life. Subscribe to your favorite preparedness vendor's catalogs or emails and buy on sale to maximize your purchasing power. A list of recommended sources is available in Appendix G. This is how my family first began to build food independence and we continue to pick up selected commercially prepared items even though we can, dehydrate, and freeze dry the bulk of our food now ourselves.

When you are ready to expand beyond commercial products, pick <u>one</u> of the preservation methods to start. I do not recommend trying to learn all three at once. Select the method that best matches your interests, food security goals, personal skills, and financial abilities.

Frankly, I recommend everyone start with canning, if you do not already have this important skill under your belt, if for no other reason than, canning is the one method you can use reliably in a grid-down scenario. You do not want to be trying to learn how to can when your life literally depends on it.

Fruits, pickled products, and tomatoes (which are technically still a fruit) are great first steps since they can be processed using water-bath canning. As long as you have a large pot, you can get started for about $15 in tools and the cost of your canning jars. When comfortable, expand into pressure canning to increase the range of foods you are able to store.

Figure 63
Water-bath canned tomatoes - a great place to start your food security journey

While canning will only provide food storage in the two to five year range, as long as you are actively canning the harvest each year, you can meet your goals using canning alone. This is the method our ancestors used – successfully, or you would not be reading this book! Supplement with commercially available products to fill in the gaps in your storage. For example, if you are focusing exclusively on water-bath canning, concentrate your purchasing on those foods that cannot be safely water-bath canned, such as meats and vegetables.

Once you have both water-bath and pressure canning skills in your quiver, continue with "I am using one or two of these methods" below to add another arrow.

I store commercially prepared foods

As I have mentioned previously, storing commercially prepared foods is where my family and many others started on their food security journey. Even as you begin to store your own foods, if the reasons you store lead you toward extended long-term storage, you should continue to augment your supply with commercial products. Shop sales. Buy items you cannot readily preserve yourself. If you are concerned about building your storage quickly, use commercial long-term storage, especially bulk items like wheat, rice, beans, and oatmeal, to fill gaps in your supply.

If long-term storage is your focus and you are looking to quickly extend your stores, you may want to start with dehydrating, rather than canning, since dehydrated foods

will store for longer intervals than home canned goods. If cost is not a barrier, considering moving directly into freeze drying as this provides you the ultimate in long-term storage.

If your primary focus is preserving the harvest or creating a hedge against inflation, canning is a great place to start, as you are more likely to want to use your food storage sooner, rather than later.

Figure 64
From left, dehydrated onions, mushrooms, and corn, packaged for short-term storage

I am using one or two of these methods

If you are already using at least one method of food preservation, you are well on your way to self-sufficiency.

Got canning under your belt? Dehydrating is a great next step. If long-term storage is your focus and costs are not an obstacle, go for freeze drying to maximize the longevity of your storage.

If you are a pro with the dehydrator, it is high time you learned to can. By now, I am sure you are well aware of the gaps in your food storage created by relying solely on dehydrated foods. Canning will allow you to extend your meat preservation, add comfort foods like jellies or relishes, and process foods in additional formats, such as chunks of potatoes and carrots, rather than only thin slices.

Alternatively, you can make the jump into freeze drying and really diversify your storage with foods like eggs, milk, cheese, and even raw steaks. Tailor your choice of method to your intended food use. I can jams, fruits, tomatoes, potatoes, and meats for short-term use. I dehydrate herbs and some of my apples because my mother likes the taste of my dehydrated apples better than freeze dried. However, since I am focused on long-term storage, I freeze dry just about everything else.

Figure 65
Freeze dried mashed potatoes make a great replacement for commercial instant potato flakes

Whichever method you choose to add to your set of skills, having two or more food storage methods greatly increases the flexibility of your food storage. If canning is one of those methods, it allows you to balance your use of short and long-term storage. Additionally, canning provides the ability to preserve food in the event of a catastrophic loss of power that will quickly eliminate other food preservation methods.

I am using all of these methods

If you are using all these methods, what are you doing reading this chapter? Kudos to you! **Now go store some food!**

WORKSHEETS

WORKSHEET 1
Why I Store

(See Chapter 1)

Worksheet for: _____

I want to build food security for my family to *(check all that apply)*:

☐ Avoid having to go to the grocery store so often *(1-week supply)*

☐ Stretch my food dollars *(1-week supply)*

☐ Store the harvest *(no specific duration)*

☐ Prepare for natural disasters especially _____ *(2-week supply)*

☐ Prepare for man-made disasters especially _____ *(4-week supply)*

☐ Prepare for short-term supply chain breakdowns in my area *(4-week supply)*

☐ Prepare for price increase of foods my family needs *(2-week supply)*

☐ Prepare for economic unrest *(13-week supply)*

☐ Prepare for regional or worldwide pandemic *(13-week supply)*

☐ Prepare for long-term degradation of society *(26 or more weeks supply)*

☐ Prepare for the aftermath of an electromagnetic pulse (EMP) *(26 or more weeks supply)*

WORKSHEET 2
For Whom I Store

(See Chapter 2)

Worksheet for: _____

Immediate Family

_____
_____

Age	How Many	Age Multiplier	Age Total
Adult (11+)		x 1.0	
Children 7-10		x 0.9	
Children 4-6		x 0.7	
Children 3 and under		x 0.5	
Immediate Family Total			

> *Remember to add 1 year to each of the children's ages before placing them into an age category.*

Extended Family

_____
_____

Age	How Many	Portion Multiplier	Age Multiplier	Likelihood Multiplier	Age Total
Extended Family Total					

Others to Help

_____
_____

Age	How Many	Support Duration (days / 365)	Age Multiplier	Age Total
Others to Help Total				

Immediate Family _____ + **Extended Family** _____ + **Others to Help** _____
= Total adult equivalents on which to base your food storage _____

WORKSHEET 3
How Much to Store

(See Chapter 3)

Storage goals for: _____

Calories per day for Immediate Family: _____ (from *For Whom I Store* worksheet)

Calories per day for Immediate and Extended Family: _____

Calories per day for Immediate and Extended Family plus Others to Help: _____

Minimum Storage Goal

Duration and for whom: _____

Calories to meet minimum goal: _____calories per day x _____ days = _____ calories

Ideal Storage Goal

Duration and for whom: _____

Calories to meet ideal goal: _____calories per day x _____ days = _____ calories

---

Intermediate Goal 1

Duration and for whom: _____

Calories to meet intermediate goal: _____calories per day x _____ days = _____ calories

Intermediate Goal 2

Duration and for whom: _____

Calories to meet intermediate goal: _____calories per day x _____ days = _____ calories

Intermediate Goal 3

Duration and for whom: _____

Calories to meet intermediate goal: _____calories per day x _____ days = _____ calories

Intermediate Goal 4

Duration and for whom: _____

Calories to meet intermediate goal: _____calories per day x _____ days = _____ calories

WORKSHEET 4
What to Store

(See Chapter 4)

Worksheet for: _____

Calculations for which storage goal: _____

Calories to store for this goal from *How Much to Store* worksheet: _____

Calculate target calories: Step 1: Calories to store x food category percentage = category total

Step 2: Category total x (1 - percent of calories provided from fresh foods)

Protein (20%):   Step 1: _____ x .20 = _____
____ % fresh   Step 2: _____ x (1 - _____) = _____

Grains (25%):   Step 1: _____ x .25 = _____
____ % fresh   Step 2: _____ x (1 - _____) = _____

Vegetables (25%):   Step 1: _____ x .25 = _____
____ % fresh   Step 2: _____ x (1 - _____) = _____

Fruit (20%):   Step 1: _____ x .20 = _____
____ % fresh   Step 2: _____ x (1 - _____) = _____

Dairy (10%):   Step 1: _____ x .10 = _____
____ % fresh   Step 2: _____ x (1 - _____) = _____

Food Preferences to Store

Proteins	Grains	Vegetables	Fruit	Dairy

APPENDIX

"Plan for what is difficult while it is easy; do what is great while it is small." - Sun Tzu

APPENDIX A
Container Inventory

Download a copy of this form from my website at http://BuildingFoodSecurity.com

Food Item	Servings	Calories/Serving	Date Stored

"A goal without a plan is just a wish." - Anonymous

APPENDIX B
Master Inventory Log

Download a copy of this form from my website at http://BuildingFoodSecurity.com

Food Group: _____ Page ___ of ___

Cumulative Calories from prior page (if any) _____

FOOD ITEM	DATE STORED	CALORIES IN PACKAGE	CUMMULATIVE CALORIES

> *"The time to repair the roof is when the sun is shining."*
> - John F. Kennedy

APPENDIX C
Vegetables
Calories per 1 ounce

Vegetable	Calories per 1 oz	Vegetable	Calories per 1 oz
Garlic	42	Red Cabbage	9
Olives	32	Chives	8
Corn	27	Kohlrabi	8
Sweet Potato	24	Mustard Greens	8
Peas	23	Pepper	8
Potato	22	Turnips	8
Parsnips	21	Arugula	7
Chicory	20	Cabbage	7
Shallots	20	Cauliflower	7
Leek	17	Eggplant	7
Kale	14	Pumpkin *(fruit)*	7
Artichoke	13	Asparagus	6
Horseradish	13	Bell Pepper	6
Squash	13	Mushrooms	6
Beetroot	12	Spinach	6
Brussels Sprouts	12	Turnip Greens	6
Carrot	11	Chard	5
Onion	11	Endive	5
Rutabaga	11	Tomato *(fruit)*	5
Broccoli	10	Zucchini	5
Winter Squash	10	Celery	4
Collard Greens	9	Chinese Cabbage	4
Fennel	9	Cucumber	4
Green Beans	9	Lettuce	4
Green Onion	9	Radishes	4
Okra	9		

"Vegetable Calories," Calories.info. Your calorie chart database: Calories for hundreds of foods, accessed September 15, 2022, https://www.calories.info/food/vegetables.

"Make preparations in advance…you never have trouble if you are prepared for it." - Teddy Roosevelt

APPENDIX D
Oxygen Absorber
Recommended Amounts

Bag Size	More Dense Foods	Less Dense Foods
	100cc: 5-8	100cc: 10-12
	500cc: 1-2	500cc: 2-3
Mylar Bag 12in. x 18in.	1000cc: 1	1000cc: 1-2
(1.5 gallons)	2000cc: 1	2000cc: 1
	100cc: 3-4	100cc: 4
	500cc: 1	500cc: 1
Mylar Bag 10in. x 14in.	1000cc: 1	1000cc: 1
(1 gallon)	2000cc: 1	2000cc: 1
	100cc: 1-2	100cc: 2-4
	500cc: 1	500cc: 1
Mylar Bag 8in. x 12in.	1000cc: 1	1000cc: 1
(1/2 gallon)	2000cc: 1	2000cc: 1
	100cc: 1	100cc: 1-2
	500cc: 1	500cc: 1
Mylar Bag 6in. x 10in.	1000cc: 1	1000cc: 1
(1/4 gallon)	2000cc: 1	2000cc: 1

More Dense Foods: eggs, milk and other food products that have been processed to a powder

Less Dense Foods: non-powdered fruits, vegetables, and meats (anything dimensional)

Reference

"Oxygen Absorbers Recommended Amounts", USA Emergency Supply, accessed February 17, 2022, https://www.usaemergencysupply.com/information-center/packing-your-own-food-storage/oxygen-absorbers-recommended-amounts.

"Prepare for the unknown by studying how others in the past have coped with the unforeseeable and the unpredictable."
- Gen. George S. Patton

APPENDIX E
Tools and Supplies Checklists

Canning

Water-Bath

❑ Pot with lid, deep enough to cover jars with at least 1" of water

Pressure Canning

❑ Modern pressure canner (not pressure cooker!)

Both

❑ Canning jars with lids and rings (see Chapter 7 for recommended sizes)
❑ Jar lifter
❑ Headspace / Bubble tool

Optional

❑ Magnetic lid lifter
❑ Reusable lids
❑ Extra jar rack

Dehydrating

Air Dehydrating

- ❑ Twine
- ❑ Paper bag (for mushrooms)

Sun Dehydrating

- ❑ Old bedsheet or screen

Optional

- ❑ Furring strips to create a frame

Oven Dehydrating

- ❑ Oven
- ❑ Cookie sheets or trays
- ❑ Fan (if not using a convection oven)

Optional

- ❑ Extra oven racks
- ❑ Oven thermometer

Dehydrator

- ❑ Standalone dehydrator, with separate time and temperature controls

Optional

- ❑ Extra trays (for stackable styles)
- ❑ Mesh liners
- ❑ Parchment paper

All Types

- ❑ Mylar® bags
- ❑ Oxygen absorbers
- ❑ Impulse sealer

Optional

- ❑ Canning jars, lids, and rings (for short-term storage only)
- ❑ Pump-N-Seal® (to manually vacuum seal jars)

Freeze Drying

❏ Freeze dryer
❏ Vacuum pump
❏ Stable, elevated foundation
❏ Bucket (to drain melting ice)
❏ Oil (for standard or premier pumps)
❏ Oil filter device (with replacement filters)
❏ Funnel (to refill oil)
❏ Used oil container, suitable for freezing, to separate oil and water
❏ Mylar® bags
❏ Oxygen absorbers
❏ Impulse sealer

Optional

❏ Silicone molds
❏ Small trays
❏ Small cooling racks
❏ Extra freezer dryer trays
❏ Silicone tray liners
❏ Parchment paper
❏ Moisture detector
❏ Tray stackers / lids
❏ Gloves (for handling frozen / hot trays)
❏ Log book
❏ Canning with lids and rings (for short-term storage only)
❏ Pump-N-Seal® (to manually vacuum seal jars)

Preparedness, when properly pursued, is a way of life, not a sudden, spectacular program.
- Spencer W. Kimball

APPENDIX F
Great Choices and
Top 5 Tips Summary

Great Choices

Canning	Dehydrating	Freeze Drying
• Jams and Jellies	• Herbs	• Eggs
• Tomatoes	• Apples	• Cheese
• Sweet Potatoes	• Fruit Leathers	• Ice cream
• Peaches	• Yogurt	• Meat (beef and pork)
• Apples and Applesauce	• Meat Jerky	• Prepared meals
• Chicken		• Fruits
• Beef		• Veggies

Top 5 Tips Summary

Canning
- Use only Ball or Kerr lids
- Do not reuse lids for canning, except Tattler Reusable Canning Lids
- Check jar and lids for imperfections before use and reuse
- Consider standardizing on wide vs regular mouth jars, based on your usage
- Use a jar packer (aka "pickle packer") to maximize fill

Dehydrating
- Store in small quantities to avoid moisture reabsorption issues
- Make sure to use the proper temperature for food type
- Test each tray for dryness – one moist piece will spoil entire package
- Rotate trays during dehydrating
- Allow extra time when humidity is high

Freeze Drying
- Use pre-freezing to lower processing times and reduce failures
- Keep bags of frozen vegetables on hand for quick "fill-in" batches
- Use moisture meter to check dryness
- Package in Mylar® with oxygen absorber for longest storage
- Re-tighten bolts on carts and other foundations supporting your unit

Better to have, and not need,
than to need, and not have.
- Franz Kafka

APPENDIX G
Resource List

Prepared Foods

Emergency Essentials   www.beprepared.com

Mountain House   www.MountainHouse.com

Augason Farms   www.AugasonFarms.com

Thrive Life   www.ThriveLife.com

Equipment and Supplies

Harvest Right Freeze Dryers
www.harvestright.com

L'Equip FilterPro Dehydrator
www.nutrimill.com/product/lequip-filterpro-food-dehydrator/

Excalibur Dehydrator
www.excaliburdehydrator.com

Pump-N-Seal®
www.pump-n-seal.com

Tattler Reusable Canning Lids
www.reusablecanninglids.com

Ball and Kerr Products
www.freshpreserving.com

Books

Ball Complete Book of Home Preserving, edited by Judi Kingry and Lauren Devine

The Complete Book of Home Canning produced by the U.S. Department of Agriculture

The Ultimate Dehydrator Cookbook by Tammy Gangloff, Steven Gangloff, and September Ferguson

Dehydrator Bible by Jennifer MacKenzie, Jay Nutt, and Don Mercer

Circumstances can force your hand. So think ahead!
- Robert A. Heinlein

Food Index

C = Canned, DH = Dehydrated, FD = Freeze Dried

Visit http://buildingfoodsecurity.com for:

- Downloadable worksheets
- Inventory forms
- An EXCEL spreadsheet inventory template

Sign up for the Building Food Security Blog!

Made in the USA
Monee, IL
26 August 2022

12598868R00096